life is sweet

333 Ways to Look on the Bright Side and Find the Happiness in Front of You

addie johnson

Conari Press

158
JOH

14.95

First published in 2008 by Conari Press,
an imprint of Red Wheel/Weiser, LLC
With offices at:
500 Third Street, Suite 230
San Francisco, CA 94107
www.redwheelweiser.com

ISBN: 978-1-57324-323-0
Library of Congress Cataloging-in-Publication Data
available upon request

Cover and text design by Jessica Dacher.
Typeset in Baufy and Exuberance Primary.

Printed in Canada
FR
10 9 8 7 6 5 4 3 2 1

The paper used in this publication meets the minimum requirements
of the American National Standard for Information Sciences—
Permanence of Paper for Printed Library Materials
Z39.48-1992 (R1997).

For Bailey and Daniel, the best happiness hunters I know.

contents

acknowledgments

Thanks to the folks at Conari for all
their help and encouragement, to Bailey
for taking nice long naps so I could write,
and to all my family and friends for the
wealth of stories and insights.

foreword

Years ago, a friend of mine shared with me the secret of happiness. It used to be on a sign at a donut shop in the Midwest. It read,

As you wander through your life, friend,
whatever be your goal,
keep your eyes upon the donut
and not upon the hole."

That's it. The more we focus on what is good and right in our lives and in the world, the better and sweeter life is. And the more we notice what's wrong, lacking, broken, or messed up, the worse we feel. It's all there, donut and hole, misery and bliss. How we feel all depends on which part we pay attention to. Simple, right?

Not so. Because so many of us are so very, very talented at embracing the hole or even insisting that the hole is all there is. Or at least, like me, falling into the hole on a regular basis for all kinds of known and unknown reasons.

That's why this book of Addie Johnson's is so important. It's chock-full of ways to make sure you stay focused on all the calorie-free donuts in your life: friends and family, nature, love, stuff and no stuff, purpose and passion. And, unlike any of my books 'cause I tend to be oh-so-serious about everything, even happiness, it even offers a bunch of jokes so you can experience the joy of laughter.

Addie is real and wise and silly, just the right companion to help you discover just how sweet life is. Enjoy.

MJ Ryan, author of
The Happiness Makeover

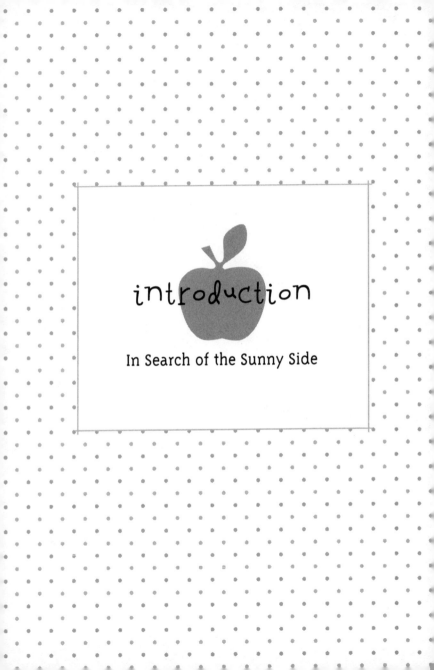

introduction

In Search of the Sunny Side

Joy delights in joy.

William Shakespere

Life is just a bowl of cherries, right? Or pears. Or maybe it's a bed of roses. All of those quaint old sayings seem to have lost a bit of their charm in the bustle of modern life. Cherries have pits and are sprayed with pesticides. Who knows what a bed of roses actually is besides a metaphor? And living life on the sunny side of the street is a sure risk for skin cancer.

We struggle with war, poverty, global warming, rising crime rates, a barrage of news, hardly any of it good. People get sick, they die, they get divorced. Civility is as rare as gentleman doffing their hats. Celebrities have fabulous lives, but you don't. And the *If only*'s threaten to take the day: "My life would be sweet if only I were richer, more famous, thinner, younger, older, had a better job, lived in a different city . . . ."

Who's happy? My friends are miserable, my family has shouted at each other through each of the last four holiday seasons, all the dogs I know are neurotic, and even the people on television are letting me down. And I don't mean the newscasters; I mean the fictional, made-up, don't-even-have-real-lives-or-real-problems people. They aren't happy either! I'm not happy a lot of the time—I worry too much, get down on myself at every opportunity, tend toward laziness and self-pity.

But before I labeled myself an unhappy lump for life, I thought I'd try accounting for all the times I notice something that makes me smile, or laugh hysterically, or walk around for a whole afternoon with a spring in my step. Maybe I am at least a little bit happy.

I have family and friends I love deeply, a husband I'm head over heels for, and I get to fill my days mostly with stuff I like to do that furthers my personal and professional goals. I am blessed to run a theatre company with some of my favorite people in the world, and lucky enough to carve a living out of acting and writing. And look, here's a bowl full of fresh fruit on the table from the farmer's market, chemical free. Happiness is all around, if I stop to take a look. Whoa, stop the presses. Or rather, start the presses—I've got a book to write.

Modern Inconveniences

Recently our apartment was burglarized and our computers were stolen. Two days after the burglary, after changing the locks and cleaning up the mess, we got on an airplane for a cross-country flight. We pulled out of the gate and sat in the plane on the tarmac for close to five hours before finally taking off for our six-hour flight. Our almost-two-year-old son was booked as an infant and was sitting on my lap, and we'd gone through all our snacks and activities by the time we got in the air. The flight turned out just fine—we all arrived safely, we were able to entertain our son, and he ran up and down the aisles until the flight attendants were cross-eyed. The upside? Now we know we could take him to Japan on a direct flight, no problem.

A burglary, losing a computer with a month's worth of unbacked-up work, an annoying air traffic control snafu . . . why am I even bringing these up? These things are not tragedies; they can't even compare to the frustrations and suffering experienced by huge masses of people around the world every day. But they are just the sorts of things that can demoralize us, chip away at our well-being, and threaten our most precious commodity—our happiness.

The Pursuit of Happiness

Through my travels, conversations, and research, I've come to the conclusion (and I ain't the first or the last to come to it, let me tell you), that after the basic needs of survival are met, the pursuit of happiness is the *most* important thing we do in our lives. Why else would we spend so much time thinking about it, making art about it, hoping and wishing and planning for it? If we're putting all that energy into happiness, why aren't we happier? Well, a lot of it has to do with what we think it means to be happy. Our definition is all screwy. Even though I know better, I catch myself at least fourteen times a day thinking about how happy I will be when I get through my dentist appointment, or deposit a bigger paycheck, or when I don't have any more stinkin' problems. And as I'm thinking those things, I fail to appreciate the little things that are making me happy right this moment. The wind in my hair, the crunch of an autumn apple, my kid's toothy smile, a great movie, a catchy tune. It's all in how I look at it—and if I'm keeping a tally, there are at least as many positives as negatives. Even better, if I want to I can tip the scales to the sweet side once in a while.

You cannot *poof* yourself happy. And nobody else can either—no fairy godmother or perfect imagined spouse, no guru or fitness instructor. If you got everything you wanted (or thought you wanted)—*poof*—right now, you'd certainly feel happy for a little while. But scientists who study this stuff, and spiritual leaders, and that wise old lady across the street all know one thing: feeling happy doesn't come from getting everything you think you want for nothing. It comes from dreaming about your goals and working to reach them. And it comes from paying attention to the little things in life that trigger a feeling of happiness—if you let them. It's great when the outcome of your efforts is what you want, but that's all really icing on the cake.

There's a ton of medical research to back it up: people who appreciate where their bread is buttered and how sweet the jam on their toast is—well, they're healthier, they live longer, they're usually more successful (although they may not define success as having the most marbles), and for sure, other people want to spend more time around them.

Buried Treasure

I went on something of a treasure hunt to create this book. I polled my friends and family. I read some new books and went back to some old favorites. I dug deep into my own psyche. As I was writing, and especially after we were burglarized, I realized that even when we're going through a tough time, or getting in a bind, we need to stay open to the reasons for happiness all around us. There's a mountain of evidence that life is sweet, if we'll just stop to look at it.

Life Is Sweet is the result of my treasure hunt: a collection of 333 things that make me—and lots of other people, including, probably, you—happy. It's chock-full of stories, vignettes, aphorisms, quotes, ideas big and little, not to mention bits and pieces from the media—all of them pointing to the same conclusion. People, stories, kids and animals, stuff/no stuff, goals achieved and unpleasant tasks done, laughing (snickering, giggling, guffawing, wetting your pants), health or progress toward it: all are fodder for happiness.

Why a list of 333 things? I could claim that a mystic oracle told me this number, and that by repeating it in a whisper while closing your left eye and stirring your coffee counter-clockwise you could have unlimited power and influence over the stock market and have reliable premonitions of the color trends for spring or the filly who's going to run away with the Derby this year. But no, reason one is about simplicity. Life is sweeter when it's simple. And a lot of the time it's the simple things that make life sweet, and 333 is a nice, simple number.

The second reason is that most people (myself included) think life can't be sweet all the time. So 333 is a nod to that eminently sensible idea. Forget sweet

365, Sunday through Saturday, rain through shine all year long. Three hundred and thirty-three gives you a few days a year to be crabby if you must.

The third reason is that while we're counting ways to see that life is sweet, what *really* counts and makes life better is developing an attitude of seeing and being the happiness *right in front of us*. And that takes a bit of practice. And 333 times is a bit of practice and then some.

Too often we hide away the treasure of our own happiness as if there's a limited supply, and we forget that life will bring plenty more booty for us. So it's time to go out looking. You'll find some right on your doorstep, some in your immediate circle of friends and family, some in the love passed among us all. You'll find some in stupid jokes, some in philosophical musings. You'll find that some treasure sneaks up from behind and finds you, and some stays hidden and difficult to seek out. But don't forget that you have the map that will lead you to more happiness than you can ever imagine, and you've had it forever—it's your birthright.

Happiness doesn't care how much money you have or the circumstances you were born into. Your treasure map goes where you go; it's printed on your face and in your fingerprints, waiting for you to unlock its potential. Have fun on your search for the sunny side, and don't forget to enjoy the journey. Life *is* sweet and creamy—yes, your life—if you just look at what's in front of your face.

one

Love and Other Forces for
Good in the World, like Giving,
Sharing, and Finding Money

We cannot do great things
on this Earth, only small
things with great love.

Mother Teresa

Love really does make the world go 'round. From teenagers in a lip lock, to old marrieds going bowling on a Friday night, to sisters who talk every day, to the friends who are so close they're really your family, to the kindness of strangers. Love is the best. It's the impetus for the creation of songs, poems, gardens, and more (not to mention babies). It's a reason for long journeys, and it keeps hope alive in the hardest places. The love between two people is a living thing with its own history and hopes, a journey in and of itself. The love in a family nurtures us and keeps us going. The love for humanity inspires generosity, growth, and understanding. And, as they say in all those songs and poems, love never dies. It is a currency that cannot be devalued, a flower that never loses its bloom. It is often the greatest comfort when someone has died to remember how they loved and were loved by others.

Passion ignites purpose, and most if not all of the forces for good in this world emanate from love: generosity, understanding, kindness, justice. Most of us are surrounded by more love that we might consciously think about on a day-to-day basis. You're on the receiving end of love that is literally flowing around the globe. Perhaps even better, you're on the giving end of that love, and no matter how much you share, the tank never runs low.

When you're down in the dumps and you think fortune has turned on her heel and walked out on you, you see a spot of green among the fall leaves in the gutter. After love, finding money is the next best thing. But more on that later.

1 Someone to Do the Work With

I remember talking to a friend at brunch and coming to one of those realization-of-the-obvious moments. We were talking about our youthful ideas of finding a mate: that when we found Mr. Right, the journey would be over. There would be minimal struggle after that, and little arguing or compromise; the relationship would exist in a kind of perfect glass bubble. Somehow we thought that our relationship with "the one" would be immune from the needs and pressures of every other relationship in our lives. Boy, were we dumb, and thank goodness. As my uncle said before he married my husband and me, "A relationship between two people in love is probably the most difficult thing God asks us to do." And he wasn't kidding. My friend and I are both lucky and thrilled to have found our Mr. Rights—the ones we want to do the hard work with from here to eternity—and that's far more exciting than any glass bubble.

2 Off to Bed and Forget the Fight

Maya Angelou's brother gave her a painting with the instruction to hang it so that it was the last thing she and her husband saw before going to bed at night. So if they were in the middle of an argument, they could look at the painting and say, "Oh, stop. Whatever it was, whatever you said, forget it," and go to bed with a twinkle in their eyes.

3 Basic Needs

"As far as living a healthy, happy life goes, I hold loving and being loved right up there with fresh air and water."

—Oprah Winfrey

4 Again and Again

Weekend trips, spring cleaning, looking at photos, long drives, finding something new for the house. Ah, the fun work of reconnecting with your partner over and over. A couple's work is never done.

5 Love Is

"Love is the condition in which the happiness of another person is essential to your own."

—Robert Heinlein

6 Shakespeare

He knew a thing or two about love. This scene from *As You Like It* always sticks with me. Phebe is a shepherdess pursued by heartsick and thickheaded Silvius. But Phebe is head over heels in love with Ganimed, who is Rosalind disguised as a man (which is why she says she can be in love with "No Woman"). Orlando is in love with Rosalind. She likes him too, but she's using her disguise as a test to see if he's for real.

PHEBE: *Good Shepherd, tell this Youth what 'tis to love.*

SILVIUS: *It is to be all made of Sighs and Tears, And so am I for Phebe.*

PHEBE: *And I for Ganimed.*

ORLANDO: *And I for Rosalind.*

ROSALIND: *And I for No Woman.*

SILVIUS: *It is to be all made of Faith and Service, And so am I for Phebe.*

PHEBE: *And I for Ganimed.*

ORLANDO: *And I for Rosalind.*

ROSALIND: *And I for No Woman.*

SILVIUS: *It is to be all made of Fantasy, All made of Passion, and all made of Wishes, All Adoration, Duty, and Observance, All Humbleness, all Patience, and Impatience, All Purity, all Trial, all Observance: And so am I for Phebe.*

PHEBE: *And I for Ganimed.*

ORLANDO: *And I for Rosalind.*

ROSALIND: *And I for No Woman.*

How's that for a definition of love from an illiterate sheepherder?

7 Love List

If I'm feeling low, one of the best ways I know to perk up is to make a love list. It's simple, just a list of every single person I love. Then I follow it up with another list, of all the people I know who love me. I can stash it in a pocket to take with me on a tough day, or just keep it in mind as I get on with my life.

8 Love Letters

Not just for romance, you can write a love letter to almost anyone. Try writing a letter full of love to your favorite aunt, or a writer you admire, or even yourself! You could also send a letter to a perfect stranger who might need some love and support—someone in the military, or recovering from a natural disaster, or coping with a loss.

9 Remembrance

I'm fascinated by family histories, and I love to hear stories about courtships, births, deaths, and strange happenings from my grandparents, aunts and uncles. I love feeling connected to places I've never lived, and to people I haven't seen in eons through the love that's been shared and passed down in my family.

10 Growing Up

Maybe the best thing about becoming an adult is a shift in my relationships with friends, family, and my husband. It's the change from the relationship being about self-validation to being about knowing. I worry less and less about how I look or feel when I'm with someone else, or what I'm getting out of my interactions, and I'm more and more focused on a genuine desire to know the people I love inside and out. I'm also more willing than I've ever been to allow other people to try and get to know me in that way, too, warts and all.

11 Green and Slimy

"Love is like seaweed; even if you have pushed it away, you will not prevent it from coming back."

— Nigerian proverb

12 Silly Stuff

I love that stuff shared between couples that seems loopy to everyone else. The word or joke or song that makes them smile moonily at each other and shut out the rest of us cranks.

13 Puppy Love

There's something wonderful about seeing a preado-lescent boy pad around faithfully after the object of his affection. There's also something wonderful about seeing a real puppy pad around after the boy he loves, totally smitten.

14 A Soft Spot

My uncle is a cop who doesn't get his feathers ruffled easily, and isn't a mushy type at all. I don't know what possessed me, but I asked him recently, "Is there any-thing that makes you giddy?" And he replied, "I don't know if I've ever been giddy. . . . Maybe young love. . . . Walking with Angela [his wife] on the beach." And my heart melted.

15 Loving the Single Life

There are plenty of people who are wonderfully happy being single, and wouldn't have it any other way.

Playing the field with no intention of settling down, or happily spending time with loved ones, they soar above the trivial dramas of cohabitation, and have often found joy through a true love of themselves.

16 Pretending to Be Strangers

I love those moments with my husband when I learn something new about him, something I might never have guessed and am surprised I didn't know sooner. Maybe the way to kick-start this feeling once in a while is to pretend to be strangers. Ask your partner to tell you a story from her childhood, or to describe a time in her life when she faced or overcame a fear. Talk like you're just meeting someone—but without any stranger anxiety—a stranger you trust implicitly to share special secrets about your past or the intriguing things about the way you think or relate to the world. Too often we forget to keep "getting to know" our partners because we assume we already know them well enough, so it's fun sometimes to start at the beginning.

17-25 Love Is All Around

Some things that make me happy when I see them:

17. Romeo & Juliet

     I love witnessing awkward teenager love, in the
     stage right before in blows up into full-scale
     Romeo and Juliet madness. When two kids are
     excited and into each other, but really worried
     (for the moment) about jumping in. Toes curled
     over the diving board, so to speak.

18. Romeo & Juliet All Tied Up

     My husband told me that he saw two teenagers
     making out on the subway, in that conspicuous
     way that only teenagers can get away with. He
     said he noticed them stop and the girl tied their
     shoelaces together, and then they promptly went
     back to happy canoodling.

19. Railway Reunions

     I like to pass the time as I wait in a train station
     by watching as someone paces, checking the
     arrivals board again and again. Then watching

as the reunion unfolds with their friend, love, mother, sister. . . . These are best when there is some running with arms outstretched, or some laughing through tears.

20. Sharing Headphones

The other day I saw a mother and her maybe six-year-old daughter on the subway, each with one earpiece, jamming out and dancing so hard to the music they were both hearing that the little girl's earpiece would fall out from time to time. They'd laugh hysterically until she got it back in and then they would go back to their boogey.

21. Bathroom Graffiti

I can't say much about what's written on the walls in men's rooms, but I do have fun imagining the histories behind some of what's written in the ladies' stalls: A+D, S+D 4ever, U unlocked my ♥ and threw away the key, Lila my love 2000.

22. Tattoos

Like bathroom graffiti, just a little more personal and probably more permanent. It might not be for you, but some people have beautiful tributes to their husbands, wives, or kids. And don't be stalled by thoughts of breakup or regret—you can always find a way to change the tattoo. Like Johnny Depp, who got his "Winona Forever" tat shortened to "Wino Forever."

23. T-shirts

Okay, so you're not ready to go under the needle? Something a bit more temporary is a cool graphic tee. You can order custom ones online, or make them yourself at specialty shops. Like "I can't stop thinking about Daniel." Or "Property of Polly."

24. Presents

I'm a fool for gift wrap, even if I'm not the one getting the present. Watching people walk down the street around the holidays with bags stuffed to bursting with colorful paper, ribbons, and bows just about sends me over the edge.

25. Good Things/Small Packages

I love seeing a man with a little bag in that telltale Tiffany blue. Just imagine the jitters he's got about whether he picked the perfect thing, and the look on her face that tells him he did it just right.

26 Keepsake

"Treasure the love you receive above all. It will survive long after your good health has vanished."

— Og Mandino

27 The Only Word We Need

"One word frees us of all the weight and pain of life: That word is love."

— Sophocles

28 Hiding Money

As a child I had the habit of stashing cash. I would slide a dollar bill in between two books on a shelf, or place a neat stack of quarters inside an empty jewelry box. Then, in the long intervals between room cleanings, I'd forget all about the money and be thrilled when I found it. And I'm not alone in this. Annie Dillard talks about hiding pennies as a kid in her memoir *An American Childhood*, and drawing chalk arrows to the hiding place with promising notes for strangers like, "Money Ahead!" What joy for the hider and the seeker.

29 Hiding a Lot of Money

There was a news story recently about people finding money in public toilets and mailboxes all over Japan. The gifts are in various amounts, but based on media reports the totals are in the millions of yen (probably more than $100,000), and some have contained a note asking the finder to do good deeds with the money. But the secret giver or group of givers remains a mystery. Some people are keeping the money, but most are following Japanese custom and turning it in to the police to be claimed. They can get it back later if nobody comes forward and then spend it doing good deeds, which seems like good karma coming and going.

30 The Love Underneath

Like I said before, scratch the surface of every good thing in the world, and you'll find love.

GENEROSITY: *Love of giving freely*

LISTENING: *Love of tuning in*

KEEPING PROMISES: *Love of following through*

FORGIVENESS: *Love of self*

PEACE: *Love beyond self*

UNDERSTANDING: *The love underneath it all*

CURIOSITY: *Love of knowledge*

JUSTICE: *Love for fellow human beings*

two

Friends, Family, and Foreigners:
Heaven Is Other People

Hell is other people.

Jean-Paul Sartre

I don't want to face the wrath of the Existentialist Society of Wichita,* so I won't go into any direct interpretation of Sartre's quote. I will just share my personal, gut reaction to it. It's sort of true. People suck. And on an even more basic level, the fact that other people exist and I am separate from them and yet around them and still really have no way to experience exactly what they are experiencing—that sucks.

However, I believe the opposite is also true. Heaven is other people. Yes, I will never really know what it's like to be my high school English teacher, or the president, or even my own son. But, as author BJ Gallagher says, "If a problem has no solution, it's not a problem, just a fact." There's nothing I can do about it; the fact of my separateness is just a fact, and the way to find heaven on Earth is to try to bridge the gap between me and everyone else through generosity, communication, shared experience, everyday rituals, and genuine curiosity. So in the name of finding nirvana, here are some

* I completely made up this organization, but if it doesn't already exist, it should, don't you think?

quotes, some experiences, some ideas, and some good old people-watching moments.

31 Inner Peace

"I believe that the very purpose of life is to be happy. From the very core of our being, we desire contentment. In my own limited experience I have found that the more we care for the happiness of others, the greater is our own sense of well-being. Cultivating a close, warmhearted feeling for others automatically puts the mind at ease. It helps remove whatever fears or insecurities we may have and gives us the strength to cope with any obstacles we encounter. It is the principal source of success in life. Since we are not solely material creatures, it is a mistake to place all our hopes for happiness on external development alone. The key is to develop inner peace."

— Dalai Lama

32 Finding Lost Friends

I recently took some time to follow up on the impulse I get every week or so to seek out people that I've lost touch with over the years. I don't know what we did before the Internet. It took only a little time to shoot a few quick emails around the country, and within twenty-four hours I had baby pictures, recent histories, and writing clips. But the interesting thing was that all three people I got in touch with had been thinking about contacting me a couple days before getting my email. It was as if I had sent out a psychic detective to people I once had a very close connection with, and before I got around to following up, half the work had already been done. So the next time you think, "Hey, I wonder what ever happened to so-and-so," you might surprise them by tracking down their email address and telling them you got their psychic message.

33-36 Family

How amazing that you belong to a group of people, by blood, by marriage, or by choice. They are your context, your root system, your springboard, and your landing pad. And you are theirs.

33. Parenthood

    It's a feeling you didn't know until that moment when you become a mother or a father, and then you can't imagine your life before you felt it.

34. Grandparenthood

    Author, educator, and humorist Sam Levenson said, "The reason grandparents and grandchildren get along so well is that they have a common enemy." It's true, these two are really in cahoots. There's something about grandkids—it's like Your Kids 2.0, and you get another chance to do all the fun stuff and can pretty much opt out of the annoying stuff when you want to.

35. Brothers and Sisters

I'm an only child, but I do find myself wishing as an adult that I had someone my own age who grew up with me, so at the very least I could turn to them and say, "Am I crazy because of me, or because of our childhood?" My husband has ten siblings from a combination of marriages and families, so he knows from what he speaks. Just the other day he was talking about how amazing it is to have people in your life whom you know you will love forever and vice versa, no matter what, even if you don't feel like putting up with them for six months at a time.

36. Aunts, Uncles, and Cousins

I always thought of these as family-lite, in a really good way. Meaning you can let down your guard and be yourself, you can have a ton of fun with them, but because you don't usually live together you probably don't end up screaming at each other about who used the last squeeze of toothpaste. Maybe they'll let you eat sugar cereal and tell you about the birds and bees, too.

37–44 Family Rituals

Most families have something they do on certain special occasions that everyone can look forward to with excitement and/or dread. It probably comes as no surprise that research consistently credits these rituals with strengthening marriages and families and imparting a strong sense of self to kids.

37. Swedish Pancakes at Christmas

My husband's grandfather's mother taught him to make these buttery masterpieces, and it's a Christmas morning treat that Grandpa's been teaching his grandchildren to make for their grandkids someday.

38. Cluck, Cluck

    In my family, we do the chicken dance at wed-
    dings. Even at my wedding, above my thunder-
    ing objections.

39. Christmas Treats

    We also do a couple sweeter things, though: my
    mom likes to read *A Child's Christmas in Wales*
    aloud at Christmas, and every year I get in
    my stocking (among other, sometimes flashier,
    gifts) a toothbrush and socks.

40. Family Reunions

    The best place to get your cheeks pinched by a
    lot of people with the same last name, and to go
    hoarse describing your year in the Peace Corps
    twenty-three times in a row.

41. Birthdays

    I think it's fun to have something you *always*
    do on your birthday, whether it's a toast in your
    honor, a special food, or getting spanked once
    for each year you've been kicking around this
    planet. On my birthday we have angel food cake

because as a kid I was allergic to dairy; and if I'm in a place that gets dark enough at night, I like to watch the Perseid meteor shower, which passes through around the same time as my birthday.

42. Date Night

Dinner, a movie, pretending like you don't have a houseful of kids and their toys for four hours straight. We don't get to do it enough, but I think having a weekly date night with your partner is the one of the best things you can do.

43. Sunday Dinner (or Monday Dinner)

Whether your family is two people or thirty, I love the tradition of getting everybody together for dinner once a week. In our family it often has to be Monday dinner because as actors we only get Monday nights off, so make it any night of the week dinner, whatever works for your family.

44. Holidays from Other Countries

Children's Day in Japan on May 5: You can play all day, and fly a kite in the shape of a koi fish.

Boxing Day on December 26: Because it has nothing to do with boxing.

Restoration of Lithuania's Statehood Day on March 11: Why not?

45 Songs from Your Parents' Generation

No matter your age, there is something wonderful about the music your parents listened to. Even if you made mean gagging sounds about it as a teenager, chances are that now you have at least a little nostalgic appreciation. Whether it's Bob Dylan and Joni Mitchell, the Four Tops and Aretha, Elton John and Iggy Pop, Frank Sinatra or Elvis Presley, it can be comforting to relive your childhood through music. What we listen to is so much a part of who we are, and what thoughts we're processing at any given time in our lives. Your adult ear can pick up things you never noticed as a kid, which in turn open up insights about your parents themselves and your relationship to them. It's a lot cheaper than therapy, too.

46 Choosing Your Parents

My parents always told me that I chose them before I was ever conceived. They especially liked to remind me of this when I was embarrassed by their behavior in public, or unhappy with a particular punishment. "You chose us, so you might as well be happy about it," they'd say. But maybe it's true. Shortly after I met my husband, we told each other about a dream we each had on the same night: of a baby boy with bright blond hair sleeping between us. Maybe that was the night our son chose us for his parents—he came seven years later.

47 The Family You Choose

I don't know what I'd do without my friends, old and new. If your family is perfectly normal and never forces you to pretend you don't know them in a restaurant, I envy you. Don't get me wrong, I wouldn't trade my band of crazies for anything in the world, but sometimes I need some time off. That's why I've got my chosen family—the godparents, aunties, and best friends who might as well be blood relations—to step in and save the day. They do, and for that I will always be grateful.

48 Kindred Souls

"Friendship is born at that moment when one person says to another, 'What! You too? I thought I was the only one.'"

— C. S. Lewis

49 U 4 U

"The greatest happiness of life is the conviction that we are loved—loved for ourselves, or rather, loved in spite of ourselves."

— Victor Hugo

50 Friends

True friendship is at the core of any happy life. If our family is our root system, our friends are our fellow branches. We're all striving together, supporting one another, providing shade and comfort.

51 How to Know If You're Nuts

"The statistics on sanity are that one out of every four Americans is suffering from some form of mental illness. Think of your three best friends. If they're okay, then it's you."

— Rita Mae Brown

52–55 Cooking and Eating

One of the oldest and simplest human rituals, we do it every day.

52. **Someone Else Cooks, You Eat**

I remember the BLTs my grandfather would make in midsummer, with fresh baked whole wheat bread with a good smear of real mayo, soft leaf lettuce, and thick slices of tomato from his garden. I forget sometimes how eating food made by someone else is an intimate experience of trust, willingness, and expectation. When it's done right, either in a five-star restaurant or your grandfather's kitchen, eating a meal someone has made just for you can fill your heart as much as your belly.

53. **You Cook, Someone Else Eats**

Our friend Sean volunteers a couple times a month at God's Love We Deliver, an organization that delivers fresh food to people living with HIV/AIDS, cancer, and other serious illnesses. He has a blast cooking food he'll never eat and making new friends of folks he might never have otherwise met in the bustling city.

54. Cooking and Eating, All Together Now!

In my house growing up, there was a standing policy of "everybody in the kitchen." At a gathering of friends and family, you could set out a plate of snacks in the living room, but it would go untouched. Everything happened at the center of the universe, also known as the kitchen. Newcomers were quickly scooped up into the action, handed a cheese grater or a colander, and many hands made quick and fun work of the meal.

55. Out to Dinner

Faced with a sink full of dirty dishes and an empty refridgerator, sometimes nothing makes me happier than going out and letting someone else do the shopping, the prepping, the cooking, and the clean up.

56–58 Tripping Out
from a Different POV

56. Mountain People, Beach People

In Italy, the population is roughly split into two camps. The divide cuts across political lines and tears through families. There are mountain people and beach people, and never the twain shall vacation together.

Now, in a country where everyone gets a month off every year, this is a big deal. Wait a minute, a month? Somebody get me a pen so I can fill out these immigration papers.

57. Go Take a Hike

It might tell you something that in the United States, instead of mountain and beach people, we have Coke and Pepsi people, but I leave that to your separate examination.

58. Happy from New Point of View

Though I've always been a beach person, I recently took a trip up into the mountains near Yosemite, California, and was pretty amazed.

They even had a lake up there with a mini-beach! So maybe there are other new things I could discover by crossing over into new territory? Coffee versus tea, red versus white (just go get me a rosé!), dogs versus cats, liberal versus conservative? It's important to remember in the midst of our most staunch beliefs, we have to make room for the perspective of those around us. Otherwise we might really miss out.

59 Remember, We're Foreign Too

On my most recent cross-country flight I sat next to an Italian couple and we talked for a good four hours. It was a nice chance to sweep some of the cobwebs off my Italian minor from college, and just to get a fresh perspective on the weirdness of the United States to someone who's never been here. The couple came through LA and toured the Grand Canyon, Las Vegas, Death Valley, and San Francisco. How's that for a combo? Then they were on their way to New York. Yep, that just about covers the United States. I think it was very confusing to them that we live in a place with such broad contrasts: between the expansive natural places and the manufactured insanity of the gambler's paradise, between the car culture of Los Angeles and the European-like San Francisco. Also, apparently, we're all putting *way* too much sauce on our pasta.

60 Getting Out There

Heaven is other people all over the world, and I personally would love to meet more of them. Do you have a top ten list of places you'd like to see (or return and see again) in your lifetime? If not, get on it. Write it down and make some plans already.

Here's my (partial) list:

1.   A good chunk of time in London
2.   Italy, Italy, Italy
3.   Iceland
4.   The Great Barrier Reef

5. The Galapagos Islands

6. Every ocean (by boat, of course!)

7. Morocco and Egypt

8. South Africa

9. South of France

10. St. Bart's, St. Tropez

11. Cabo San Lucas, Mexico

12. Tuscany

13. Carmel, California

14. Ireland

15. Prague

16. Japan

17. New Orleans

18. The headwaters of the Mississippi

Wait, did I say top ten? Oh well.

61 The Magic of "How"

Do you get nervous talking to new people? Someone once told me about a little trick that helps me when I feel like crawling into the wallpaper at a social gathering. Instead of "yes" or "no" questions, ask questions that start with "how." You can ask it about almost anything, starting from the get-go, like, "How did you get your name?" "How" questions take the pressure off you because they take longer to answer, and usually they lead to an interesting story or conversation that will break the ice. When you know someone better, questions like, "How do you feel about that?" and, "How did you make it through that situation?" extend an empathic olive branch that allows you to deepen your connection to your friends.

62 Crazy Fruit Guy

On my lunch break I used to go every now and then to a man with a sidewalk cart selling fruit. I know nothing about his story, but he was like the Dr. Jekyll and Mr. Hyde of guys who sell fruit. Some days he was so sweet to me—smiling as I walked up, throwing in a couple extra cherries, chatting about the weather.

And other days he was a real grump. One day he flat out refused to sell me a banana. He looked at me from top to bottom, stared at my feet as if I was standing in a pile of monkey manure, and then waved me away with a sigh. I tried going with my glasses on, or taking them off. On one of his bad days, I tried giving him a tip, which let me tell you was a disaster. I tried to piss him off by giving him a $20 bill for a 35¢-banana, and because it was one of our *simpatico* days, he didn't flinch as he fished out my change.

I'll just have to chalk it up to this: the fruit guy feels how he feels. He makes no apologies, and no attempt to hide his feelings. And perhaps more important, he can let it go and feel entirely different the next day. And even if it is due to some semi-psychotic state brought on by eating too much fiber, I think we can all learn something from this guy. Honor your feelings, for real, and don't worry what people will think of you. Why not?

63 How Customers Are Made Happy

Another fruit guy was on a corner on the opposite end of town, and he just made me smile. I gave him a ten for $3.50 worth of plums, cherries, and almonds, and he gave me two quarters from his fanny pack, one dollar from his right front pants pocket, and one five from the middle of a neatly folded wad of bills in his back pocket. It was a little change ballet, and after he was done he smiled and said, "I don't want to give you all ones. Customers are not made happy by all ones."

I thought it sweet that he thinks it through like that, and that he concerns himself with how customers are made happy, or not, in the littlest ways. And that he's made himself into a living cash register, with a different spot for each bill and coin.

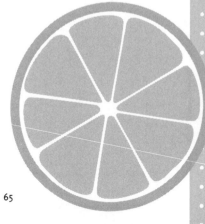

64 Other People

If hell is other people and heaven is other people, it looks like we have a choice. Sometimes you'll want to be a loner, and sometimes you'll want to be a joiner: at school, at home, at work, in your neighborhood. You get to decide how to maximize your happiness.

three

Kids and Animals: Keeping Up
with Whippersnappers, Fur Balls,
Scales, and Feathers

I have been studying the traits and dispositions of the "lower animals" (so called) and contrasting them with the traits and dispositions of man. I find the result humiliating to me.

Mark Twain

Kids and animals? Do these two things really go together?

"No!" says the crazy cat lady in apartment 1 H, who would snatch a tuna fish sandwich out of her grandson's mouth to give it to her twenty-plus roaming felines.

"No!" says the mother of the poor allergic child whose third goldfish just went belly up.

"Yes!" say I, if only because the warm-cuddly, isn't-that-funny, aw-shucks feelings I get around pets is only slightly weaker than those same feelings elicited by kids. Both animals and kids can make us happier (with, in some cases, bouts of frustration or even sheer misery). Some people's happiness is so intertwined with their pets' that they want to spend eternity scooping the litter box in the hereafter; several historical figures have been buried with or next to their pets, just like people with their kids. So, you may not yet be convinced, but kids and animals can provide happy moments by the bucketful. Come to think of it, they can provide dirty diapers and manure by the bucketful too, but that's a different story.

65 Creature Comfort

There are tons of studies about how animals make us feel better. Dogs and cats in nursing homes help patients live longer and feel happier, and I just read an article about dogs predicting earthquakes and other natural disasters. It seems our love for animals goes back to a prehistoric mutual connection. Somewhere along the line, we figured out that animals' heightened perception can warn us of danger way before we know anything about it. So, if you live in a mineshaft, you're going to want a canary hanging around. If you live in wolf country, it might be nice to have a big, loud dog. And if you live in an apartment in the city, it will still make you feel warm and cuddly to be greeted each evening with a friendly meow when you walk in the door.

66 Purring

Did you know scientists still aren't sure exactly what purring is? We hear it when we're scratching that special spot, but cats do it when they're agitated or hurt, too. And one crazy theory I've read is that purring is in a range of sound frequencies that can improve bone density and help muscles heal, thus contributing to the famous nine lives of our feline friends. I suppose tying a cat to your plaster cast to help heal a broken bone might have a downside or two, but still, I can't help but wonder if kitties' healing powers are communicable.

67 Happy Bird-Day

I knew a cockatiel once who could sing (well, whistle) "Happy Birthday." He often sang it when he was nervous, like when new people came to the house. I should say, he could whistle *part* of "Happy Birthday"—so it went something like this (without the words, of course):

Happy Birthday to you,
Happy Birthday to you,
Happy Birthday to you,
Happy Birthday to you, . . .

It was pretty charming, and also slightly maddening, but the best part was watching people's changing reactions. First, delight that a little bird was whistling a recognizable tune. Second, amusement that he kept getting stuck on the same spot. Next, nervousness as they wondered how long it would go on. And finally outright annoyance at hearing twenty minutes of the first measure of that damn song over and over and over again.

68 Am I a Crazy Cat Lady?

Okay, you've pinned me, I'm something of an animal freak. The only kind I don't like are the ones that skitter in front of me from gutter to garbage can on a steamy summer night in the city. Yep, I can live without city rats. (I actually don't mind the cute white ones that people keep as pets. I know, double standard.) You can keep your cockroaches, too. And maybe chickens—I'm not their biggest fan. But I digress. Animals of all kinds, wild and domesticated, I just love 'em.

69 Man Felled by Small Orange Fur Ball

My husband once got to spend an afternoon with two tiger cubs. They were maybe 20 pounds each, max, and he described them playing and lounging and eating. When he got up to leave the room, one of the cubs lunged at him from behind, hitting right at the bend behind his knees and taking him down to the floor instantly. He didn't know what hit him. He said he realized in that moment how perfectly attuned those animals are for hunting in the wild. That even at a couple months old, raised in captivity, the cub had the instinct to strike in the right spot with enough force to playfully catch a human six times his size.

70–76 Animals in Motion

When I'm stressed out, I take a minute to produce my own internal nature program. Here's how it works: Close your eyes and imagine a scene (or several scenes) of animals doing what they do best. See it in slow-mo, or aerial view, or extreme close-up.

77 The Animal Perspective

I met a woman recently who's an animal communicator; that is, she talks to animals and they speak to her in the same way you and I talk to our therapists. She told me a story of visiting a turtle who was unhappy in his new home. The turtle's concerned owners gathered around to witness a deep reptile-human encounter. When she leaned down to the turtle's cage to ask him what was wrong, he said, "You have a big head." I'm not sure if he meant it in the metaphorical sense or was just stating the obvious, that her head was bigger than his whole body. But either way, she thought it was pretty funny.

78 Teeny Tiny and Utterly Massive

The blue whale is the largest animal on Earth. It's as big as a jet plane, with a heart the size of a small car. Fifty people could stand on its tongue, though I'm not sure I would elect to be one of them. And they eat some pretty small critters called *krill* by the ton to keep up their bulk.

There is something magical about scale, isn't there? Almost the whole planet is teeming with life of every imaginable size, from the microscopic organisms that groom our eyelashes for us to the miles-wide groves of genetically identical aspen trees growing out of the same root system. The differences between us humans, or between my waistline now and five years ago, seem pretty unimportant in comparison.

79–81 Legendary Dogs

Most families I know have at least one legendary dog in their history. Somewhere in their last three generations, there's a canine who stands out as especially talented, smart, or funny.

Here are a couple I know:

79. The Farm Dog

    My dad's childhood dog Lady was a German Shepherd-Collie mixed breed. She was the perfect farm dog, and could bring the cows in for milking by herself if necessary. Once, my great aunt fell and broke her hip in the pigpen, and Lady defended her from an angry pig. Didn't know pigs will come after you when you're down? Yep, some will.

80. The Baby-Sitter

    Fritzie was a German Shepherd who lived with my godmother in the '60s, when her youngest daughter Nora was around a year old. It was the days of playpens, and in the small town where they lived it was safe to leave the baby in her playpen on the front porch for a minute or two. The dog would lie down in the shade of the nearby bushes, keeping close watch. Nora would gurgle and giggle and coo at passersby, and when they started up the path to say hello to the baby, Fritzie would lunge at them, snarling, and they'd run away in a panic as baby Nora laughed and laughed. Then Fritzie would head back to the bushes and Nora would get ready to lure in the next unsuspecting stranger. Tricky Fritzie.

81. The Horn-Dog

My husband's dog as a kid was Bilbo, named after C. S. Lewis's famous hobbit. He was known for being incredibly horny, and therefore an expert escape artist. He would break out of his kennel and go on the prowl, and have to be tracked down again, detached from his lucky (or unlucky) lady dog, and put back in the new and improved kennel. This happened several times, with the fence getting taller each time. When the fence got to be seven-feet-high, Bilbo learned to climb it. As they constructed a roof for his kennel, he learned to tunnel his way to freedom. You've got to admire the spirit—anything for *amore*.

82 Animal Shows on TV

It is a fairly common event in my household for my husband to come home and find me on the couch, surrounded by tissues and mid-sob as I watch any of the animal shows.

83 The Three-Hanky Movie

I think this all started when I was introduced by my mom's friend Jean to Lassie movies, which she always rated according to how many handkerchiefs you needed to mop up the tears as you watched them.

84 Best Friends

A dog will be there whenever you call, always be thrilled to see you come through the door, sit by your feet (or on them) through your darkest moods, jump at the chance to join you whenever you go out. What could be better?

85 Dolphins

Did you know that there are no confirmed cases of dolphins attacking humans in the wild, but there are many stories of dolphin pods shepherding humans out of the path of hungry sharks?

86–89 Pet Names

A source of never-ending joy to me is the names people give to their pets (or in some cases, the names the pets earn themselves). Here are the good, the bad, and the hairballs.

86. Famous People

It's always fun to have a VIP in the house, if only in name.

My friend Polly has a goldfish named Gwen Stefani (I'm in favor of always giving goldfish last names, and also middle names where appropriate).

Howard Stern and his girlfriend Beth Ostrosky have a bulldog named Bianca Romijn-Stamos-O'Connell, after their famous model friend, her ex-husband, and her current husband.

Or you could call your pooch Mr. Famous, like Audrey Hepburn's Yorkshire Terrier.

87. Themes

If you have more than one dog or cat, you might consider making them all-of-a-kind in name by picking a theme like the ones here. If you have more than one fighting fish (and you want to keep it that way), keep them in separate tanks.

Musical instruments: Banjo, Dulcimer, and Fiddle

Ice cream flavors: Mocha, Caramel, Banana Split

Weather: Thunder, Snowy, Rainbow

Colors: Red, Brownie, Blue, Old Yeller (though I'm not really sure if this dog was named for its color or its bark)

Shakespearean characters: Oberon and Titania, Falstaff, Hamlet

Martha Stewart has four dogs: Beethoven, Mozart, Verdi, and Vivaldi

88. "That's Sure Different"

I'm all for slightly odd names.

President FDR's beloved Scottish Terrier had the full name Murray the Outlaw of Falahill (shortened to "Fala").

Lord Byron's favorite pet was called Boatswain. And why am I not surprised that Rudolph Valentino's Irish wolfhound was called Centaur Pendragon?

89. Pet Names—Enough Already

Puns: Virginia Woof, Charles Barkley, Bing Clawsby, Lady Bird Johnson

A fake pedigree name: Absolute Artemis Armani, Silver Noodles Trickster

Anything that will embarrass them (or you, for that matter): No really, dogs have self-esteem too. I read somewhere that dogs are very sensitive to the social cues of humans. I don't know who figured this out, but when dogs get to know their name, they pay attention to how it is used, and if it makes people laugh or tease them, there may be long-term ramifications.

90 Kids and Cloud Nine

I'm not going to go into the crazy things people name their children for fear someone's going to come after me. But now, on to the kids! Children, like animals, can ground us in reality, reinforce a sense of purpose, and remind us how to live the good life.

91 The Puppy-Baby Matrix

Babies: adorable. Puppies: delectable. Puppy licking baby's face with tail wagging furiously until baby laughs so hard she falls down? It just doesn't get any better. Babies + Puppies = Cutefinity.

92-94 An Epidemic of Children Hugging

On my street in Brooklyn, I recently witnessed three special hugs. And I'm sure there have been countless more that I don't know anything about. Okay, I know that isn't exactly an epidemic, but a mini-something?

92. Hug Number One

First I saw a two-year-old run up and throw his arms around a complete stranger. The man crouched down to the ground and said, smiling and laughing, "God bless you, God bless your future." As I walked by I could tell that man had needed that hug. And getting it brought tears to his eyes. The two-year-old, of course, just trucked on down the block as if nothing special had happened. All in a day's work.

93/94. Hugs Number Two and Three

Then I was walking down the same block yesterday in a terrible funk. Two sisters, maybe six and eight years old, were standing at their door waiting for their grandmother to catch up and open it. "Hi!" they yelled in unison, and the smaller girl rushed up and threw her arms around my waist. Being an adult who lives in the modern world, I had no clue what to do, so I awkwardly patted her on the back, but I couldn't help smiling.

Then the older girl came up, and this time I was ready to bend down and give her a real hug. It took three hugging kids for this one bleary-eyed adult to get the point and just give and take the simple pleasure of a hug for no good reason. "Bye," we all waved, and went on about our business.

I know, I know. We can't teach our kids to go around hugging strangers. That wouldn't be safe.

But sometimes, kids can sense more about the world and the people in it that we give them credit for. And sometimes people just need a hug.

95 The Best Age

Our friend Mark works part time as a baby-sitter, and when I asked about the kids he sits for, his eyes lit up as he talked about the "little, little babies." He loves working with newborns; it's an age that he just clicks with. Sometimes I hear a parent say, "Oh, (fill in the blank) is a tough age," or "Get ready for four, you're in for a treat." Which leads me to believe that those of us who like hanging out with kids often have a "best age." (Except those of us who think any age kid we're around is the best age. This might be another one of those the-world-is-made-up-of-two-kinds-of-people splits.) And maybe the universe made us this way so we can pass our kids around to willing and able helpers at each stage of their development. Like they say, it takes a village.

96 The Joy of Teenagers (Seriously)

Now, most people would say that the teenage years are not their idea of a best age. Surly, secretive, hormonal, confused. Maybe they bring back memories of our own tortured adolescence. My father was one of those people who had a string of best ages—he was a kid magnet, but teenagers might have topped the list. He worked for years in an adolescent psych ward, and found humor and joy with some of the most troubled teens imaginable. Come to think of it, my mom really likes teenagers too. I guess I got lucky. If you can sit back and pull yourself out of the inevitable power struggles, I can see how watching a child push through into young adulthood could be pretty exciting. It's also a good time to practice the challenge of setting limits that are free enough to let them take responsibility, but not so loose that they are set adrift.

97 Your House, Your Rules

Kids give us maybe the greatest chance we'll ever get to look at our own attitudes and actions with fresh eyes and make the changes we feel we need to. Think about the rules you want your kids to live by—do you live by them? Honesty, hard work, a good dose of play every day, playing fair? You tell them that actions speak louder than words, or to follow their dreams no matter what, or that you love them no matter how mad you get. Are you giving yourself the same unconditional love? The best parents I know really mean it when they say, "I just want my kids to be happy." When's the last time you held yourself to that standard—for your kids or yourself?

98 Acting Like a Baby

What would the world be like if we all acted like babies, at least emotionally? Babies are excellent communicators long before they can talk. Adults are not always great receptors, but that's another story. Their crying isn't only about communicating; it's about going through the emotion fully, and physically getting it out of their system. Then the slate is clean for the next learning experience as it comes down the pike. What a great way to live—it almost makes you want to be a baby again. On second thought, never mind. I like to choose my own outfits and use the potty like a big girl.

99–105 Through a Child's Eyes

What other cues can we take from the kids around us besides honoring our unbridled emotions?

99. What Things Mean and How They Work

Why do we have to move on from the "why?" phase of life? Sure, it can get annoying when the response to every single thing you say is "Why? Why? Why?" But we could all stand to ask "Why?" a little more often.

100. A Fanatical Love of Trains, Dogs, and Ponies

"A dog! A dog! A dog! A dog!" my son yells until I acknowledge that yes, there is a dog coming down the sidewalk toward us. What makes you so excited you want to shout about it in public?

101. Playing Dress-up

When's the last time you put on your best costume jewelry and threw a tea party?

102. Sharing

It's tough to share sometimes, but the results can be rewarding in unexpected ways.

103. Attention to Detail

Every puddle deserves a thorough investigation.

104. Acceptance

Seeing everyone with fresh eyes, on equal terms.

105. Doing Things Just for the Sake of Doing Them

Jumping jacks, silly faces, knock-knock jokes, holding hands, sticking peanuts up your nose. Okay, scratch that last one or you might end up in the emergency room on the pointy end of a pair of pliers.

four

Healthy, Wealthy, and Wise:
Balancing Push-ups and Popsicles,
Ohm and Omigosh

It is health that is real
wealth and not pieces
of gold and silver.

Mahatma Gandhi

We'd all probably like to be healthier than we are; many of us could stand to eat less and exercise more, and too many of us suffer from stress, lack of sleep bordering on exhaustion, or both. Even when our life-style doesn't lead to serious disease, we have a nag-ging feeling that things could be so much better if only we could get a little more rest, make it to the gym or the park more often, and eat healthier.

Then again, most of us (myself most definitely included) would not be happy leading a monastic life, abstinent from so much of the bad stuff that feels so good. A friend recently spent seven days in complete silence and eating a restricted vegan diet at a Zen monastery. After nearly losing his mind on day two, he settled into the routine. But he did have to sneak away and walk three miles to a local inn, where he pointed at the menu and nodded that yes, he would like the meatloaf please. At the end of his stay, when he was speaking again, he asked one of the monks how they ever survive on their limited diet. The monk confessed that they all piled in their minivan about once a month to go eat steak.

Balance is the key to good health and a good life. We do best when we're able to weigh doing what we love against doing what's good for us, and we've hit the jackpot when we can do things as often as possible that are rewarding in the moment as well as later on.

106 Meditation

More and more scientific studies are confirming the benefits of the relaxed mindfulness of meditation. However you choose to do it, through prayer, yoga, mantras, or just sitting quietly, you're probably altering your body and brain for the better. And even if you're skeptical about the physiological plusses, there's certainly no harm in taking some time alone to reflect on the day's happenings.

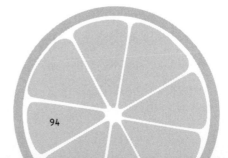

107 Walking

I grew up living next door to a close family friend, a kind of auntie figure who would invite me, and sometimes the rest of my family, over for dinner at least once a week in the summertime. She and her husband took their dog and went out walking every night after the sun went down. It was a small town with few streetlights, and once your eyes adjusted to the darkness, it was a wonderful feeling walking off the heaviness in your stomach, listening to the din of courting insects, and looking in on scenes from the lives of the neighbors through their bright picture windows.

108 Stretching

I'm a stretching wimp, I'll admit it. I'm fairly limber by nature, so I've got myself fully convinced that I don't really have to stretch. I realized the error of my ways when I tweaked my back pretty badly doing a normal, everyday activity. As I lay in bed for two days, I made a mini-pact with myself to take up some simple stretching and strengthening exercises I could do every morning for twenty minutes, and within a month my back felt much better.

109 Massage

When's the last time you had a massage? Better yet, when's the last time you had three massages in some sort of regular sequence, like every two weeks or once a month? This is the best way to do it. The first one might be uncomfortable—it gets the kinks out, and you'll probably be a bit sore afterward. The second one will start to feel better, and you can move beyond the aches and pains into some deep relaxation. By the third one you're in heaven, the toxins are out of your muscles, the energy is flowin', and you're on cloud nine.

110 Gossiping

I know, I know, your mother was right when she told you not to gossip, but what about a new take on it? Why not get together and have a feel good gossip party, where the "omigosh" is not so much about scandal, but about celebration of the great things in your friends' lives?

111 Sweet Tooth

To indulge, or not to indulge? Chocolate is one of life's great treasures, and that's just the tip of the iceberg-sized sundae. Plus, you never know what's coming next. Like Erma Bombeck once said, "Seize the moment. Remember all those women on the *Titanic* who waved off the dessert cart."

112–114 Good Things Come in Threes

A shout out to ice cream. Gelato, sorbet, milkshakes, soft serve, Popsicles, frozen yogurt, sprinkles on top, any and every flavor. However you crave it and eat it, ice cream is on any list.

112. Ice Cream Story Number One

My son is two, and for those of you who know what that means, I thank you for your sympathies. And to my mother: I'm sorry I was two once, too. So, in my weaker moments as a mother I have been known to thwart a tantrum with an ice cream cone. Recently we were on a shopping trip and he was tired (I didn't realize how tired) and I could see the thunderclouds gathering over his little head. My mother-in-law made a mad dash to the ice cream counter, and the squall was diverted, but two minutes later we looked down at the stroller and saw this: a pudgy cheek smashed into a melting puddle of vanilla, eyelids closed, even a faint snore. Now, that's good ice cream.

113. Ice Cream Story Number Two

We didn't have a camera to catch the moment with my son. Not so with my grandmother; she caught my uncle using his bowl of cake and ice cream as a pillow on one of his early birthdays, and shared it with all her grandchildren so that we could suitably make fun of him whenever we got the chance.

114. Ice Cream Story Number Three

I went for a walk the other day with my friend David, and the walk turned into a snacking tour of the city. After we'd sampled bagels, fried dumplings, organic iced tea, and artisanal cheese, we were ready to top it all off with—you guessed it—ice cream! We trekked a good long while to his favorite spot, where they make amazing gelato in unexpected flavors. I had corn and mountain blackberry smothered in fresh whipped cream. Later, I mapped our path on the 'net to track our mileage: almost four miles of eating adventures, at which point the dollop of calorie guilt I'd been feeling pleasantly vanished.

115 Tiramisu

Speaking of desserts, you know tiramisu, that delicious Italian dessert with ladyfingers dipped in espresso and smothered with custard and chocolate shavings on top? If you've never had it, get thee to a bakery whose name ends with *-ino's* and order a big slice with a canoli or two on the side. Then buzz around town with a nice little sugar rush for the rest of the afternoon. If you're a tiramisu connoisseur like myself, maybe you already know that there is a nice direct translation for the word in English. *Tira* means "pick," *mi* means "me,"and *su* means "up." It's a pick-me-up!

116 Mental Tiramisu

So, there you are in the middle of the afternoon at work. Your eyelids are down around your knees, you just called a female customer with short hair "sir," or you can't remember what your boss asked you to do five minutes ago. Besides running out to the local pastry shop, or even to the vending machine in the hallway, what to do? You need mental tiramisu. Sugar free, quick, and guaranteed to work.

Get up and move a little. Go to the bathroom, splash water on your face, and come back to your desk. Or try these ways to perk up:

117 Mental Tiramisu Remix

You know how the right side of your brain controls the left side of your body and vice versa? Well, you can stimulate your brain into thinking harder and more creatively by doing some simple exercises that cross the center line of your body, like touching your left ankle with your right hand, or putting your left hand on your right knee. Or even better, kicking backward with your right heel to *thwap* your left hand and then clapping three times as you slap your right buttock with your left hand and . . . Have I gotten you fired yet? I hope not. But maybe by now you're laughing (or being laughed at) and that's bound to lighten the mood around the workplace.

118 More Mental Pick-Me-Ups

Another trick to get the cranial juices flowing is to practice your Spanish verbs, or recite the one sonnet you remember from high school, or even just think of ten words that rhyme with *train*. Anything to mix up your routine and send your brain a signal that it had better pick up the pace and get with the program.

119 Your Personal Assistant: Your Brain

You know that moment when you can't remember your neighbor's name, or the photographer you just read about, or the date the Magna Carta was signed? You can say to yourself (out loud or under your breath, your choice), "Excuse me, brain? I know what date the Magna Carta was signed, I just can't think of it at the moment. Could you get back to me on this one?" And within twenty-four hours, I swear the answer will come to you while you brush your teeth, or in a dream, or even in a newspaper article you decide to read.

Then you can feel very smug for accessing the wealth of knowledge hanging around your semi-conscious brain.

120 The Fountain of Youth?

If you want to keep a spring in your step and a twinkle in your eye, all the while keeping senior moments and other more serious memory lapses at bay, one of the best things to do is to change your routine. Drive a different route to work, switch your right and left hands for everyday activities, eat dessert first, and wear your pajamas to work. Wait, no, that last one will get you locked in a home with a diagnosis of Alzheimer's for sure.

121 Gratitude

Your mother taught you to be polite, to say "please" and "thank you," to wait your turn, to share with others.

And by now those things are ingrained and you don't even have to think about it to remember to do them. But when's the last time you said "thank you" out loud for the good things in your life?

You can be measurably happier if you take the time every night to write down five (or more) things you are thankful for. They can be one word, or longer descriptions, or a combination of both. You have to actually do it—get a little notebook and put it next to the bed and go for it. I know you're tired, but it's worth it. If you don't believe it works, there are studies to prove it. Google it and look it up yourself. Or don't bother to Google it, just trust me and go get a pen.

122 Weigh Your Options

Somebody once pointed out to me the inverse relationship between fast food and exercise: you always want fast food, but you feel like crap afterward, while you never want to exercise, but you feel great afterward.

123 Now and Laters

When I was a kid I used to love these little candies called Now and Laters. They had two fruit flavors and went from hard to soft as they warmed up in your mouth. You get it: they're good both now and later. A lot of things we do either suck now and are great later (like potty training your two-year-old, or getting up at 5:30 a.m. to run on the treadmill), or they're fabulous now, but really suck later (like indulging in that third pitcher of sangria with the gals on a work night).

Instead of eating a plate of onion rings, or conning yourself into going to the gym, maybe it's time to find some things that are great both now *and* later. So, get out your friend Mr. Pen again and figure how to tip the balance in your life toward the good Now and Laters.

You like the results of exercise, but not the treadmill—is there another activity you might look forward to that would give you the same kind of benefits? Maybe try hiking, yoga, a rock-climbing wall, or cross-country skiing. Are there ways to minimize your occasional fried food indulgences without going cold turkey? Sure there are; you just have to make a few little changes.

124 Stick-to-itiveness

Stick-to-itiveness. How's that for a word? And I didn't even make it up, they were talking about it way back when, see?

"The three great essentials to achieve anything worthwhile are, first, hard work; second, stick-to-itiveness; third, common sense." —Thomas A. Edison

It's a great word but an even greater idea. Many of history's best success stories are thanks to sheer perseverance. Some people even think stick-to-itiveness will take you further than being talented, smart, or born rich. I tend to agree.

125 Exercise and Stick-to-itiveness

Let us just say that consistency is not my strong suit when it comes to carrying out an exercise plan. I can get really excited, and go gung-ho for the first three or four days, and then I get my master's and doctorate in excuse making. I had my husband laughing silly when I told him (after five days of doing yoga, lunges, and sit-ups in the morning) that I needed to change my routine because it clearly wasn't working. My belly was still flabby in just the way that annoys me, and I clearly needed to change things. He reminded me that I actually had to do the plan for a while, not just think about it. So, back to the yoga mat for me with an earnest determination to enjoy it even before I see results.

126 Lifelong Stick-to-itiveness

My mom was recently hanging out with a ninety-five-year-old friend who'd been a dancer, teacher, and social worker most of her life. My mom was feeling a bit sorry for herself as she got older, and the woman said something along the lines of "I know what you mean, I had to give up doing headstands at eighty-six because I thought I might fall, but I can still do the splits. D'you want to see?"

127 Spinal Alignment

Get thee to the chiropractor and come out feeling like a million bucks.

128 Taking the Stairs

"A man's health can be judged by which he takes two at a time—pills or stairs."
— Joan Welsh

129 Seeing Anew

There are lots of magic tricks and scientific studies that prove that if we expect to see something, we will pretty much see what we expect, even if it's not really there. The same thing happens in our lives: we see the same thing every day, and we shut off the part of ourselves that's on the lookout for the new and interesting, so sometimes we pass it by altogether. Can you vow to see something new every day?

130 On the Lookout for the New and Interesting

My godmother made that resolution. She thought she'd open her eyes and really see something new and inspiring every day, something that would enlighten her and lift her morale. The first day she went into the world with her new resolution, this is the scene that greeted her: she drove up to the hospital where she works, and as she sat at the stop sign, watched a man scrutinize himself in the plate glass window. "Is he contemplating his existence?" she thought. "Tracing the lines of his face and remembering his past?" Then he opened his palms, face up, spit on each of them, and slicked back his hair with the gobs of spit. She laughed herself silly. The thing about opening your eyes and seeing something new is that you never know what you'll get, for better or worse.

131 Making Choices, or at Least Feeling Like You Are

Powerlessness might just be the worst feeling we humans can face. When we're imprisoned physically, emotionally, or even in our own minds, when we can't choose our own destiny, we're in trouble. This is the stuff of binge drinking, murderous rampages, and dyeing your hair blue just to see what it feels like. Seeking out choices and making good ones will always make us happier. And for those times when there seems to be no choice, try looking at the situation from another angle. There's often a hidden, gratifying choice in there somewhere.

132 Hope

"He who has health, has hope. And he who has hope, has everything."

—Proverb

133 Positivity

Did anyone ever tell you the glass is half-full? Somebody told me once it depends whether you're pouring or drinking. Seriously, though, if you can figure out how to get optimistic and stay that way, you're home free. I'm not saying your problems are over, but simply looking at the world through rose-colored specs means that half your problems will look like exciting challenges, and the other half you'll probably realize aren't problems at all, just facts of life.

134 Drink a Glass of Water

Speaking of glasses half-full, did you know that 50 to 65 percent of your body weight is water? So you yourself are literally half-full, plus some. Only problem is, you're always losing it—sweating, breathing, peeing. Getting dehydrated can cause all kinds of problems, starting with being cranky and ending with keeling over. My mother is quick to remind me that if you are thirsty, you are already dehydrated. So hoist a full glass of the clear stuff whenever you can. And if you're flying, it's even more important—I read somewhere that you can lose up to two pounds of water on a three-hour flight. I wonder if I could drop a dress size if I went to New Zealand.

135 Sing the Blues

"For me, singing sad songs often has a way of healing a situation. It gets the hurt out in the open into the light, out of the darkness."

— Reba McEntire

136–142 Quick Fixes

Feeling blue? The singing didn't work? Here are a couple more ways to feel better fast:

136. Do the Crossword

    Stimulate your brain and feel a sense of achievement, or if you can't finish it, use it as an excuse to call up that old know-it-all uncle of yours.

137. Indulge in Aromatherapy

    Lavender, chamomile, citrus, elephant dung (just seeing if you were paying attention). Smells are some of the most powerful stimulants and soothers.

138. Try Color Therapy

    Orange peps you up, green calms you down, and silver is mentally cleansing. Get out your paintbrush.

139. Get Upside Down

    Do a handstand up against a wall like you did as a kid (though I assume no liability for any resulting aches and pains). Or if that's too intense, just try to touch your nose to your knees by bending down from a standing position. Hang there for a while and let the blood rush to your head. Reverse the effects of gravity for a moment.

140. Stop Worrying about Your Health

If you've got a mole that's bugging you, or symptoms that bother you but don't seem to add up to any particular illness, go see your doctor. If she says there's nothing wrong, make a follow-up appointment for a month or so. Then you can monitor your symptoms and she can run tests again if that makes sense. Then you can stop wasting time day to day worrying about something that's not in your control.

141. Get Some Sunlight

Get out there and boost your vitamin D. My husband's grandmother swears by sitting in her lawn chair for twenty minutes every day.

142. Enjoy that Fruit 'n' Fiber

You might think this is gross, but my uncle swears that regularity is the key to happiness. Besides, eating fruit and getting enough fiber tastes good if you do it right, and it will make you healthier, and thereby happier.

143 Spending Time Alone

"Being solitary is being alone well: being alone luxuriously immersed in doings of your own choice, aware of the fullness of your own presence rather than of the absence of others. Because solitude is an achievement."

— Alice Koller

144 Going Out Dancing

Salsa. Two stepping. Line and square dancing. Hippity-hop, as my grandmother likes to say. Even if you're way past that college/post-college phase of going out clubbing to drink too much and hook up with hotties, you can still have a blast going out with your best friends for a night on the town. Loud music + exercise + adrenaline + mild social anxiety = guaranteed mood elevation.

145 Pace Yourself

Why is it that we rush through the good stuff (hugs, walking the dog, meals) and linger over the not so good (hours of solitaire at work, reading bad news in the paper, waiting to get the car fixed)? Time to reset the internal speedometer.

146 Wisdom

"Be happy. It's one way of being wise."

— Sidonie Gabrielle

five

Laughing It Up: A Grain
of Salt Goes a Long Way

I am so clever that sometimes
I don't understand a single
word of what I am saying.

Oscar Wilde

Okay, so life's got you down. You just walked through a rainstorm with a hole in your shoe. When you got to work, you had a pretty little pink slip sitting on your desk. Your cat swallowed your favorite necklace and is going to need some expensive surgery. That guy you've been dating just told you he's in love with your best friend and that they're having a baby. Things have gotten so tragic, it's almost funny. Well, actually, if you were writing a screenplay of your life, it could go either way.

And why not? People in the worst situations still find a way to laugh. In fact, some would argue that we need laughter most when we're at our lowest point. They say laughter is the best medicine, to which I would also add it's the best way to bond with friends, the best pick-me-up, the best ice breaker, the best tension diffuser, and the best way to get through tough times. So have a giggle or a chuckle, a chortle or a snort, and get on with it.

147 Laughing at Yourself

You know the type; they make the perfect straight man in comedy. Persnickety, controlling, stiff. I catch myself in this mode and I have to laugh. Then I swing back the other way, to the wild, goofy child poking fun at my uptight self.

148 Two Types

"Some cause happiness wherever they go; others whenever they go."

— Oscar Wilde

149 Sound Advice

"Always act your shoe size."

— Anon

150 More Laughing

Somebody told me that an average kindergartner laughs three hundred times a day, while an adult averages seventeen times. This makes me want to be a kindergarten teacher.

151 The Playground

I love to watch kids on the playground screaming with laughter about the silliest things. Completely invested in make-believe worlds, totally in their bodies, and overflowing with sensory awareness—that's the way to live.

152 Nothing But the Truth

"My way of joking is telling the truth; that is the funniest joke in the world."

— George Bernard Shaw

153 Fake News

We think that telling the truth has to be a sober, newsy event. The most refreshing comedy tells some kind of truth, and I've read that a large percentage of people under fifty would rather get their newsy truth from something like *The Daily Show* or *The Onion* than from a more traditional source. Maybe you get better information from honest satire than from disingenuous "real news."

154 Making Connections

"Laugh. It is the quickest bridge between strangers and the finest path between friends."
— Mary Anne Radmacher

155 Horror Films

My husband loves them, but they frighten me so badly I have to sleep with the lights on for a week. He loves the weird humor of them, and even better than laughing at the bad acting in the movie is laughing at me squirming in my seat.

156 Me + Scary = Comedy

It all started the summer my husband and I met. We went to see the movie *The Sixth Sense* with a bunch of people. There's a scene in the movie where the little boy is being pursued by a ghost, and he hides in his homemade fort in the living room. The ghost starts to pull at the tent, and as the clothespins holding it together popped off one by one, I clutched my future husband's coat, twisting it so hard it started to tear. As the ghost girl stuck her head in the tent and puked, I screamed and somehow got under the seat in the theatre. Sure, it had been a mildly scary moment in the movie, but my scream was so over the top that the mood in the theatre changed as everyone fell out of their seats laughing at me.

157 Playing Your Part

"I think of life itself now as a wonderful play that I've written for myself, and so my purpose is to have the utmost fun playing my part."

— Shirley MacLaine

158 Laughter Is the Best Medicine

Common folk wisdom has always prescribed laughter for any number of ailments. The modern study of the healing properties of laughter owes a lot to Norman Cousins, a scientist who prescribed it for himself. Diagnosed with a rare disease and given only months to live, he checked himself into a hotel room and took massive doses of vitamin C and watched funny movies and television shows all day long. And it worked. For every ten minutes of belly laughs he got two hours pain free. He lived far beyond anyone's expectations and ignited more serious study of laughter as medicine.

159 Did You Know?

Laughter can boost blood flow as much as light exercise or drugs that lower cholesterol. A recent study showed it can decrease your chances of keeling over from a heart attack.

160 Guess What Else?

There's some good evidence that laughter can boost the immune system, as well as clean toxins out of the lungs and blood stream.

161 Uniting the Brain

In order to get a joke, we need to use both sides of our brain: the left hemisphere understands the verbal content of a joke and the right figures out whether it's funny or not. So laughing keeps our brains young and fit.

162 Painkiller

Laughter releases endorphins that are more potent than equivalent amounts of morphine. What's more, you don't need to go to rehab to quit laughing if you get hooked.

163–172 Funny Stuff:
A Brief Survey

163. Physical Comedy

For those of us who get a kick out of people getting knocked around, falling down, and getting heavy things dropped on them.

164. Bodily Functions

We all do it, so why is farting so darned funny? Not to mention boogers and burps. I know a kid who will laugh for twenty minutes straight if you just look him in the eye and say, "Poop!"

165. Disguise and Mistaken Identity

From Shakespeare to Steve Martin. An oldie but a goodie.

166. Men Dressed as Women

The common ingredient of some of the funniest movies ever (think *Some Like It Hot*). And my dad's best Halloween costume. He went once as his Cousin Pearl (whom he made up). At 6 foot 4inches, in a floral muumuu, construction boots, full beard, curly wig, and big, pink plastic pearls, boy, was he a sight.

167. Fruit

Slipping on a banana peel, bobbing for apples, wearing a hat made of tropical fruits.

168. Verbal Comedy

If physical comedy is lowbrow, I guess verbal is highbrow. Won't Howard Stern be pleased to know.

169. Puns

Aaagh! I have a love/hate relationship with puns. They make me laugh when they're thoughts inside my head, but out in the world, all they ever get me is a groan and an eye roll.

170. Jokes

One of life's great pleasures, I like them dumb, silly, witty, dirty, and wry.

171. Satire and Parody

A change in perspective can shed some new light on old stuff. Or just make you laugh.

172. Malapropisms

Using the wrong word to great comic effect, like in *Calvin and Hobbes* when Calvin says, "I'm so smart it's almost scary. I guess I'm a child prog-eny." Hobbes replies, "Most children are."

173–176 Funny²

Then there are the by-products of laughter itself that are funny:

173. Snorting

Best when totally involuntary and quite loud.

174. Oops

The women in my husband's family have been known to laugh so hard they pee themselves, which in turn makes everyone (including them) laugh even harder.

175. The Wrong Tube

Laughing so hard milk, or whatever else you're drinking, comes out of your nose.

176. Can't Stop! Can't Stop!

That feeling when your ribs ache and you wish you could just think about the exchange rate or global weather patterns and knock it off, but you just can't stop laughing. And because you can't stop, you're forced to repeat numbers 173–175.

177 Saint Lawrence

If you feel you need spiritual help in strengthening your funny bone, you might pray to Saint Lawrence. Patron saint of comedians, he was martyred by slow roasting on an iron grill and partway through is said to have proclaimed, "You can turn me over now, I'm done on this side."

178 A Broken (Funny) Bone

My husband has a very high threshold for pain, and when something actually does hurt him, the only way I know is if he starts to giggle. I don't know why, but in his case laughter is an automatic response to pain. Maybe it's like that theory about cats purring—his body is just getting the healing process started as quickly as possible with a chortle or two.

179–185 Fun with Water

Some of my most memorable funny times, both as a kid and an adult, have been in and around water.

179. Slip 'n' Slide

Have you ever been on one of these things? It's a long yellow sheet of plastic and you put a hose at one end and then laugh yourself silly watching people slide off the plastic and get grass stains on their faces.

180. Bathtub

My son could turn into a prune every night playing in the tub for as long as we'll let him.

181. Diving

Especially the infamous cannonball.

182. Body Surfing

Especially when your best friend comes up after a big wave with a bikini full of sand.

183. Surfing, Boating, Snorkeling, Scuba Diving

Outdoorsy types tell me all this stuff is lots of fun, and I believe them, but see number 186 for my water skiing experience.

184. Water Balloon Fight

I'm a pacifist, but this can be a full afternoon of military exercises of the best kind.

185. Fishing

You better bring some jokes along, or this could get boring.

186 Ski Ballet

I never learned to water ski, but I spent two days trying my darnedest, and entertaining everyone in the boat quite a bit. I've pretty much blocked out the memory, but I'm told I would get up on the skis and then with a kind of undignified grace slowly keel over and face plant into the fast-moving water. Like I said, I was determined to try my best, so I performed this sequence of events probably thirty times over the course of two afternoons before throwing in the towel. That's a lot of belly laughs for those folks in the boat, so at least somebody benefited.

187 The "Water Take"

I went to the School of the Arts, a public high school in San Francisco, and if you've spent any time in the city of SF you may know that the autumn months are the hottest. Yeah, it's great—foggy and cold all summer and then you get back to school and roast in under-ventilated classrooms. One hot day in acting class, our teacher Mr. Rayher had a novel idea for dealing with his group of unruly, sweaty teenagers. We all went outside and he taught us the "water take," which is similar to a standard double take, that linchpin of slapstick comedy, only with water shooting out of your mouth. We spent the afternoon setting up believable situations in which we could be caught off guard in the middle of taking a big drink, and then spitting water all over the place, getting soaked, and laughing hysterically.

188 Hurtin' Albertan

This is the nickname of Brian Utley of Calgary, Alberta, who just won the national cannonball championship in Toronto. Yes, the dive kind of cannonball where you hit the water in such a way as to make the biggest splash possible, and in the process, turn your skin bright red by slapping it into the water at high speeds. From the pictures I saw of this esteemed event, some people thought they could win the competition with gimmicks: tutus and wigs, superhero capes, and such, but Utley is a big guy, and he seems to have taken the simple approach: legs crossed with hands on knees, eyes tightly closed. A true professional. Hitting the water, he said, felt like slamming into a wall. You are the champion, my friend!

189 Ha-has and Hairballs

Did you know that animals have a sense of humor? Even laugh? I once saw a video of a crow falling beak over tailfeathers down a snowy hill, landing at the bottom covered in white fluff, shaking it off and then marching right back up to the top to do it all over again. And I guess all animals play the game I thought I invented for my cat when I was seven, the "I-I-I-I'm gonna get you" game where I chased him around the house. By the end of it we both plunked on the couch with our tongues hanging out, and nobody bugged my mother for a good fifteen minutes, which I'm sure she appreciated. But apparently rats play the "I-I-I-I'm gonna get you" fake-chasing game and chirp with delight. Nothing has gone further to rehabilitating the sullied image of that creature in my mind. Sure, they passed around the bubonic plague, but they giggle!

190 Home Videos

I can't reveal the source, because her sister would kill me, but my friend has a videotape that could easily win big bucks on one of those send-in-your-home-video shows. In the tape, she's maybe ten and her sister is four or five, and it's the end of a long day at the playground. Their mother is behind the camera and calls out, "Go help your sister down from the monkey bars; it's time to go." As my friend holds on to her sister's legs trying to get her down, she accidentally pulls her sister's pants down, at which point everyone starts laughing. The little sister laughs so hard she starts to pee, right on my friend's head. My friend screams and runs away, leaving her poor sis dangling with her pants around her ankles, midstream. The best part? Mom just keeps on taping.

191 A Good Laugh, A Good Cry

When I was ten I got the giggles with my cousin Amy. We could not stop laughing, and it went on for close to an hour. Every time we thought we'd stopped, we caught another look at each other and started right in again. Only trouble was, was we were at my grandfather's wake. Luckily he would've gotten a big kick out of our antics, so our parents felt okay about our strange expression of grief.

192–194 Road Trip Hilarity

Some memorable highway signs:

192. Are We There Yet?

    "Absolutely Nothing Next 22 Miles" proclaims a sign on a dirt road.

193. Decision, Decisions

    A sign at the end of a road, where you have to turn one way or the other: The left arrow points to "College," the right arrow points the way to the town of "Weed." Decisions, decisions.

194. A Detour Worth Taking

A highway exit sign with an arrow pointing up and to the right that reads "Climax High Point."

195–199 Ba-Dump-Dump Ching!

Now for a few jokes.

195. A Little Kid Learning to Tell Jokes

As told by a four year old:

What do you call a sleeping elephant?

I don't know. What do you call a sleeping elephant?

A sleeping elephant!

Other jokes told by small children:

What color is a burp?

Burple!

What weighs six tons and wears glass slippers?
Cinder-elephant!
What do you call a short psychic who escaped
from jail?
A small medium at large!

196. Jokes That Don't Make Sense

These are way more fun for the teller than the listener. But then the listener has an incentive to go out and pass it on.

What's the difference between an orange?
Why did the elephant paint his toenails red?
So he could hide in cherry trees!

Knock-Knock
Who's there?
Hula.
Hula who?
"p!"
Get it? Hula Hoo-p!

197. A Couple More for Good Measure

What do you get when you cross an elephant and a rhino?

Hell-if-I-know.

How many son-in-laws does it take to change a light bulb?

My mom says never mind, she'll just sit there in the dark.

What do you call cheese that doesn't belong to you?

Nacho cheese!

198. The Best Blonde Joke

I got an email a long time ago with this joke, and I don't remember the numbers because I used to be a blonde myself, but here goes:

A blonde walks into a Manhattan bank and explains that she'd like a $2,000 loan for her trip to Europe. The manager explains that they'll need some kind of collateral, and she offers her car, a brand new Mercedes parked outside. The manager is confused but she insists, so they sign the papers for the loan, she gets her money, and he drives the car into the secure underground parking lot in the building. The bank manager tells his employees, who have a good laugh at the dumb blonde. Two weeks pass, and the blonde returns and repays the loan plus interest in the amount of $7.62. The bank manager can hardly contain his snickering as he goes to fetch the car, and can't resist asking the blonde, "I'm sorry, Ma'am, but why would you leave a $50,000 car as collateral for a $2,000 loan?" And the blonde replies, "Where else can I spend $7.62 to park my car in Manhattan for two weeks and expect it to be there when I get back?"

199. My Dad's Favorite Joke

Well, he had quite a few faves, but this is the only one I can think of that I wouldn't blush to repeat in print.

How do you catch an elephant?
You dig a big hole and fill it with ashes, and then you carefully line it with peas. When the elephant comes up to take a pea, you kick him in the ash-hole.

200 Favorite Jokes

The kind of humor we respond to says a lot about us. Well, sort of. I guess you have to be somewhat mature and/or educated to get satire and political humor, and they say it helps to be immature to appreciate physical humor, but I know plenty of old, smart people who love to watch people get kicked in the rear or fall down three flights of stairs. My favorite, though, is discovering a streak of humor in someone you never would have expected. Like when your prim Aunt Shirley tells you a good raunchy one and then saunters away snickering to herself. Or when the cop who's pulled you over for speeding tells you a silly knock-knock joke he heard from his kid, just to lighten the mood.

201 Funny Laughs

I love hearing a distinctive laugh and wondering how it got that way. My friend Phoebe wheezes so loudly that people around her have been known to call for an ambulance. My friend Brooke has a laugh that goes up a little musical scale and right back down in double time.

202 Loosen Up

I don't know about you, but I'm happiest when I'm relaxed, full of endorphins, surrounded by good folks, enjoying the moment, and have clear nasal passages. Since these are all aftereffects of a good laugh, it seems that happiness is only a laugh away.

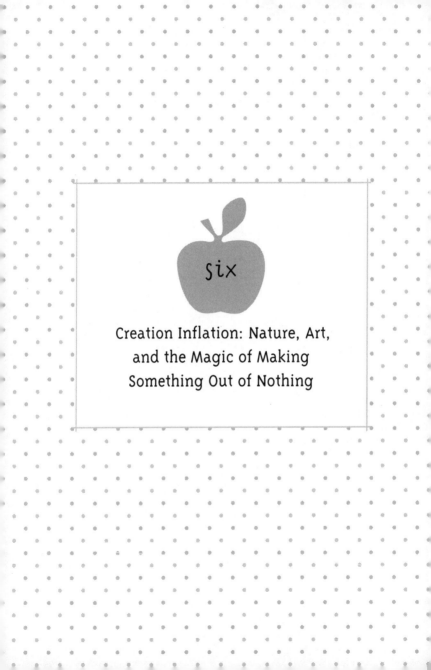

Six

Creation Inflation: Nature, Art,
and the Magic of Making
Something Out of Nothing

Creativity can solve
almost any problem.
The creative act, the defeat
of habit by originality
overcomes everything.

George Lois

The spark of creativity is life's first and greatest gift to us; we're conceived in that spark. And we have the chance to create every day, even in how we look at the world around us. We also get to bear witness to that spark in others through literature, scientific discoveries, music, and painting. If we pay attention, we can notice it in nature all around us: a perfect spider web, the formation of ice crystals on the windowpane, even a close examination of our own animal natures. Creation brings us joy, awe, and often a much needed new perspective.

An act of creativity changes everything. Change can be a source of anxiety in our lives; we wonder how we will manage each new task or difficulty we face. But if we can embrace change as constant growth through creation of new things, we can be comforted and inspired by the unexpected. The masters of artistic expression show us this better than anyone. They turn words into worlds, musical notes into stories, brushstrokes into feelings, and they change our lives in the process. I can't think of a better definition of magic.

We're surrounded by beauty of all kinds. It can perk us up, calm us down, and even heal our bodies and souls. Getting attuned to this splendor is a great way to pass the time. It's time to shine up your sense of wonder and see the world in a new light. Make some new discoveries, and don't forget to pass them on through the magic of your own creativity.

203 Butterfly Hunting

"Happiness is a butterfly, which when pursued, is always just beyond your grasp, but which, if you will sit down quietly, may alight upon you."

—Nathaniel Hawthorne

204 A Yen for Water

Every couple of months I get a yearning to go out on a boat. I'll take anything—a sailboat, canoe, rowboat, ocean liner, even the Staten Island Ferry, one of my favorites. The sound of waves on a boat hull calms my mind, and the smell of clean water and open air makes me happy.

205 Blue Water

Having grown up in and around muddy rivers and greenish ponds in the Midwest, I never quite believed that water could be blue. Then I went to the Caribbean as an adult and was bowled over. I spent every day, all day, in water that looked like a swimming pool and felt like a bathtub, teeming with brilliant colored fish and coral. Now I have a photo of the sand and sea and sky on my computer screen, to remind me whenever I need it, just how blue water can be.

206 Polar Bear Swimming

I have to admit I have never taken a plunge into icy water like they do in Polar Bear Clubs around the world. Maybe I should try it, because even in more tepid waters I do like the moment my warm body hits cold water—the rush to my head and feeling like I can hardly breathe, and then exhilaration as every skin cell comes alive.

207-210 Gardens

I think gardeners are artists, scientists, even alchemists. They channel light and water into a canvas of plants, trees, and flowers, and create a landscape for every mood.

207. Planting a Tree

There may be no better thing you can do for yourself or the Earth than to plant a tree every year. I also love the tradition of planting trees on a special occasion like a birth, marriage, or as a memorial. It creates a memory for you and your family, and greens up the world we live in, too.

208. Green Thumb

Ah, the feeling of good clean garden dirt so thick under my fingernails that no amount of scrubbing will get it out.

209. Botanical Gardens

The best-kept secret of many cities, they're like plant museums.

210. Secret Gardens

I believe that the best gardens have something hidden, a surprise dahlia around the corner, or a little pond full of fish at the bottom of the hill.

211 Horizons

I took classes once with a brilliant clown named Michael Fields, who told us to always look at the horizon—to get our eyes up off of the ground and put our focus far out in front of us. He meant it in the context of being on stage, but I'm sure he knew the value of this perspective shift in everyday life as well. Of course you can't keep your eyes fixed off in the distance, you're going to look at other things, make eye contact with a passerby, notice something shiny on the path ahead of you. But make the horizon your default position, and you will interact with the world in a different way. And it works . . . as your eyes travel to the top edges of the mountains in the distance, or the architecture of rooftops, or a flat expanse of open water, you open yourself up to seeing outside of the little bubble of sensation that surrounds you.

212 Public Land

"Everybody needs beauty as well as bread, places to play in and pray in where nature may heal and cheer and give strength to the body and soul."
— John Muir

213–216 It's Elemental

Each of the elements has its own wonders, and here are just a few to start your list.

213. Earth

Cliffs, caves, buttes, valley farms, rolling dunes, pebble beaches, pine forests, the smell of damp and slightly rotting things. Lying on the grass and searching up into the night sky.

214. Air

Birds in flight, strong spring winds, the smell after a thunderstorm, the dry heat of a desert, the thin air on mountaintops, morning mist rising from valleys.

215. Water

Fog pouring through the Golden Gate, torrential downpours, ocean waves, rushing rapids, Niagara Falls, rainforests, wetlands full of birds.

216. Fire

Crackling logs in the fireplace, fireflies, hot sun on your shoulders, mushrooms growing on a burnt tree trunk, candlelight, summer barbeques, shooting stars.

217 A Wish a Minute

The best time to see shooting stars that I know of is the Perseid meteor shower, which happens sometime during the second week of August. At its peak, on a moonless night away from city lights, you can see one to two shooting stars every minute. Imagine all those wishes coming true.

218 Collecting Shells

What's better than the ritual of beachcombing? Shoeless, with pant legs turned up, hunched over, picking through to find the shape and color that catches your eye, that tells a story. Then bringing the loot home to wash it, look it over, and lay it out in your kitchen or backyard.

219 Collecting Rocks

As a kid I collected rocks, but not semi-precious, or shiny, or even very interesting ones. My favorites were of the plain, rough, grey variety, culled carefully from my godparents' driveway. I'm not sure now what I was looking for, but I could spend hours going through the rocks one by one and picking my favorites to take home.

220 Cairns

Manmade rock formations, cairns come in all shapes and sizes and are erected for many reasons, including as memorials, at the summit of a mountain, or to mark a path through rocky terrain. To me they are a symbol of communication between human beings across incredible time and space—no fiber optic cables, satellites, or even tin cans required.

221 Mini-cairns

My godmother Margaret makes cairns in her home from rocks she collects on walks, doing yard work, or as gifts from her many grandchildren. They're all over the house, and you can almost feel the thoughts, memories, and care that went into making them.

222 Bugs

Okay, if we're talking about bugs that make me happy, those would be the bugs that are outside my house more than any I might find inside my house. I'm even happy to tip the balance by escorting any and all spiders outside on a newspaper covered with a plastic cup. I don't smush them, because somebody told me they're good luck. Bugs as part of the ecosystem, bugs making honey and silk, bugs eating peskier bugs, and so much more. It's a good exchange for those twelve mosquito bites I get every summer.

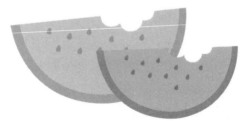

223 Free for All

Did I mention lately that nature is free? We could certainly spend a lot more on protecting it, but experiencing the natural world is a joy that doesn't have to use up a single penny out of your piggy bank.

224 Art in Nature

There are several artists whose work focuses on making temporary or more permanent art out of natural, found elements. I worked with an art teacher once who told me about the Zen exercise of picking up all the fallen leaves under a tree and then spending the time to place them down on the ground again "as the tree would have done it." What an amazing intersection between natural and human creative endeavors.

225 Music

"Music is the language of the spirit. It opens the secret of life bringing peace, abolishing strife."

— Kahlil Gibran

226 Your Soundtrack

In high school my friends and I used to sit for hours making mixed tapes for each other. Now it can all be done with a couple of mouse clicks, but the impulse is still great—to share the soundtrack of your life with someone you love. As you play it, it becomes shared background music for both your lives.

227 Marching to Her Own Drummer

I went to see Bob Dylan in concert last summer, and as you might imagine, the audience made for pretty fabulous people watching. My favorite, though, was a woman who did a sort of dance-march back and forth between two sections of seats—it was a combination of power walking, modern dance, and the moves of a souped-up baton twirler. She knew if she kept moving the security guards couldn't stop her, so she just made her way back and forth, back and forth, smiling and waving at Bob and the audience as she went.

228 Poetry versus Jingles

I'm mortified. I was just folding laundry and realized I was singing a cell phone jingle. It wasn't just running quietly through my head, either—I was actually vocalizing it! *Aaagh.* The ad men and women of this world have me wrapped around their little fingers. Time was when people memorized bits of poetry and folk songs and hummed those in their down time. Well, I say it's time for a smack down. Poetry versus jingles. A jingle on repeat annoys me to no end, but when the poetry wins out, even a couple lines of it can lift my spirit, the more repetition the better.

229 Memorize a Poem

The only way I can think to stop the jingles and other inane things in my head (including the voices of cartoon characters with British accents) is to get something better in there, post haste. When I was a kid I spent a long weekend with one of my best friends out in the country at her grandparents' house. On day two, with no television, we explained to my friend's grandma that we were bored. She laughed. Okay, she said, and offered us a dime for each poem we could memorize. I asked her if Shel Silverstein counted, she told me he did, and we were off. We each memorized a few poems, picked out a nice handful of candy in town, and it was only later on that I realized I had spent two full days reading poetry, looking for suitable things to memorize, and then performing some poems for the eager audience of my friend's grandparents. And I'd had a lot of fun doing it.

230 Infinity and Imagination

The full reach of infinity may be beyond our imagination, but imagination itself is infinite.

231 Lighting Candles

There's something very special about a touch of fire at the tip of a candle bringing light, warmth, company. Almost every culture has a special festival featuring candles or lights on or around the darkest days of the year. We make wishes on candles at our birthdays, too. They seem to have a special power in our psyche, and yet they are so simple. Delight in your favorite candle ritual today—in the bath, at dinner, outside on the porch.

232 The Real Thing

I'm sure art historians might disagree, and I can't find who said this originally, but someone told me this quote when I was still a teenager, and it has never left me: "Every revolution in art is a return to realism." It makes sense to me. Even the most abstract painters are looking for a way to express their vision of the world in the most real way possible. And the only way to do something truly revolutionary is to see the world around you for what it really is, and try to express that to others.

233 The "Aha!" Moment

Whether in science, art, poetry, history, or anything else, there is magic in new discoveries. Research has found that the majority of discoveries, even those that seem to come out of the blue, come from rearranging information that is already well known. It's like taking a thousand-piece puzzle and assembling it all out of order and yet ending up with a perfectly clear picture no one's ever seen before. Eureka!

234 Free Art

Check out the free day at your local museums, create your own walking tour of public fountains and sculpture, browse through gallery exhibitions as though you were shopping for a new Matisse for the den. And if all else fails, it's always fun to spend a rainy afternoon at the library surrounded by illustrated books: how-to books, art history books, picture books, and kids' books about art.

235 An Old Lady Color-Coordinated Outfit

Have you ever seen members of the Red Hat Society— a group of senior women wearing purple outfits and red hats? It started with a poem about wearing purple when you're an old lady, and now it's a full-blown invasion of grannies in red hats.

Anyway, I think we should all spend at least one day a month in a monochrome outfit, old lady style. Here's how: you wake up in the morning and think,

"Oh, yeah. Today's definitely an orange day." Then you proceed to take everything out of your drawers and closets that is any and every shade of orange and put it on. That's it, put everything on. Stop only when you must in order to avoid physical discomfort (like wearing three sweaters is not a great idea). The clash between different shades of orange may be a bit jarring at first, but never fear, you'll get used to it.

236 A Sense of Purpose

A friend just told me about a study she read about that showed that prisoners who are given a small animal to care for, or are offered the chance to make art in their cells, are something like 60 percent less likely to return to committing crimes than those who are not allowed to express their creativity in these ways. You don't have to be in lock down to find meaning in providing love and care to small things, and we all could find renewed purpose and direction in our lives through following our creative impulses.

237 Dance

Watching it is grand; doing it's a thrill. And do you have any idea how many calories it burns? Flexibility, strength, coordination, stamina—in tests of overall athleticism, dancers tend to rate higher than professional athletes.

238 A Mirror Up to Nature

Hamlet tells the actors who are about to perform his play that "the purpose of playing . . . was and is to hold as 'twere the mirror up to nature." I believe that all art holds up this mirror. It shows us our true selves, and even when it infuriates or bores us, we're getting a message about our place in the world.

239 Healing Color

I know someone who swears that looking at a particular Mark Rothko painting will cure any headache. The colors in his paintings seem to vibrate in shades that travel out from the canvas, so it wouldn't surprise me at all.

240 A Little (Different) Kitchen Witch

My mom's a little superstitious. But I'd never known her to have a Kitchen Witch—one of those straw figures a lot of women keep in their kitchens that (allegedly) make the kitchen a little more cozy, a little warmer in winter, cooler in summer. Kitchen Witches also prevent pots from boiling over, soufflés from falling, oven fires, things like that.

So I was home helping my mom clean up her basement after a little bit of a flood. We rescued everything important and found some things we had both forgotten about, including a very detailed drawing of a witch flying on a broom, signed "Addie Johnson, age 9" in the bottom right-hand corner. We laughed at it, and I forgot all about it.

The next time I visited my mom, she had a new addition to her kitchen. There she was, my old drawing on yellowing sketch paper, all gussied up in a very ornate, oversized gold frame (bought at a discount store, of course), hanging proudly in my mom's kitchen, where she is to this day.

The thing that really makes me happy about Kitchen Witch is remembering how happy I was to have made her. Remembering that my mom liked her so much that she saved her. Remembering the happy look on my mom's face when she found a drawing she'd forgotten all about. And picturing her hanging in my mom's kitchen, watching over the preparation of a lot of good food.

Wow—one kid's art project and at least five things to be happy about.

Seven

Stuff, No Stuff, Double Stuff:
The Thrill of Abundance, the Glory
of Simplicity, and Trashing
Our All-or-Nothing Attitude

It isn't what you have, or who
you are, or where you are,
or what you are doing that
makes you happy or unhappy.
It is what you think about.

Dale Carnegie

Sometimes I throw myself a little pity party. I stay in bed and eat popcorn and watch trashy television, thinking about everyone who has it better than me and how hard my life is. And before too long I have to laugh. I don't have it so bad at all; in fact my life is pretty great, but I find that if I indulge in feeling sorry for myself once in a blue moon, I can usually face whatever's bringing me down with a renewed spirit.

The thing is, I can think of people who have everything they could ever want and are still miserable. I can think of people just scraping by whose joy for life overflows onto everyone around them. What you think about really can be the key to happiness, and this includes how you think about your circumstances, whether they are meager or bountiful. Sometimes we take for granted the great pleasure we can take from very little things. Sometimes, too, we forget to give ourselves permission to enjoy over-the-top abundance, as if we somehow didn't deserve it. Most important, life is best when we set our judgments aside and savor the moment of whatever it is that the universe is dishing out, in big or small servings. When we have an all-or-nothing attitude, we're always coming up short (or bearing an unfair burden). Why not trade in that mindset for one that brings contentment with whatever we have right here, right now?

241 Everyday Joy

I took a poll recently of my friends and family about what's making them happy these days. And though many of them have gone through trying times, or had some big let-downs lately, nobody told me that were dreaming about some special fairy coming down to sweep away their problems. They didn't say they needed to win the lottery, or take a trip to Europe, or make some major change. I was quite touched because they all shared very simple things, things they had access to nearly every day of their lives. They talked about sailing, laughing with their kids, getting on the exercise bike, praying, a good cup of coffee, sunflowers and peonies in the garden, letters from friends, dancing alone, and freshly laundered sheets. Turns out what really makes us happy may be much more basic than the things we fantasize about.

242 Zero In on Satisfaction

Do a little exercise where you pinpoint a thing or two that makes you say to yourself, "Darn, this is good stuff." Watching your kite lift off into the air. Rowing your dingy to the middle of the mirror-still lake. Or, you know, driving your Maserati around hairpin turns on a mountain road (or dreaming about it).

243 The Cup o' the Irish

It could even be something simpler—for me it's Irish breakfast tea. The Irish, man, they aren't kidding around. This is by far the strongest, blackest tea I've ever tasted, and it's almost like they threw a bit of well-roasted peat moss into the mix. I try not to drink three cups every day, not only to avoid getting the shakes from all the caffeine, but also because I find if I take a little break, say a week or two, between indulgences, it's even better when I pick up the habit again. Absence makes the tea grow stronger, I guess.

244 Delicacies

I like fresh sweet corn in season. I like foie gras. Their deliciousness seems unaltered by their respective effects on my pocketbook.

245 Cheap Thrills and Cheap Chills

Speaking of my pocketbook, more often than not I open it up and am shocked to find it a cavern of lonely emptiness. Maybe I'm exaggerating a bit, but in any case, what's a girl to do if she can't afford a good time? Here's a start for your own list of cheap thrills, as well as some cheap ways to chill out.

246–254 Cheap Thrills

246. Going sledding

247. A pickup game of basketball

248. Buying someone a single rose and/or getting a single rose

249. Driving with the windows down on a curvy road with your favorite song blasting

250. Going wedding dress shopping (even if you're already married or have no intention of getting married anytime soon)

251. The free day at the museum, botanical garden, boardwalk, aquarium

252. Eating chocolate chips right out of the bag

253. Enjoying the view at the top of a high building

254. A downhill ride with faulty bicycle brakes (okay, scratch that last one)

255-264 Cheap Chills

255. Warm milk with honey
256. Collecting pinecones or autumn leaves
257. Fishing (or getting a stick and a bit of twine and pretending to)
258. Knitting (or getting some sticks and a bit of twine and pretending to)
259. Putting pictures in an album
260. Tossing a ball around
261. A day of drawing or watercolor painting in the park
262. An ice cream cone
263. Children's playgrounds (yesterday I saw a woman with no kids there , swinging and smiling to herself)
264. Skipping rocks

265–270 A Few More Low-Budget Pick-Me-Ups

265. Juggling

One summer my dad taught me the basics of three-ball juggling and gave me a little book as a reference. An only child with no sibling distractions, I probably spent eight hours out of the day in my room or the back yard throwing balls and dropping them, throwing and dropping them. Weeks later I started to really get the hang of it, and to this day I can pick up three small objects to entertain myself and any small fry who happen to be around.

266. A Perfectly Boiled Egg

Whatever your preference, hard or soft or somewhere in between, there is a sweet spot for your perfectly boiled egg when all factors of temperature, humidity, timing, and the phone not ringing in the middle of fixing it come together. Sit back and enjoy.

267. Juggling Three Perfectly Boiled Eggs

But wait, there's more! Those things are hot when they come out of the pan, even after you've rinsed them in cool water. So you might get to practice your juggling, too. Good thing you made three, in case one doesn't make it to the table.

268. Food Glorious Food

I can't even do it justice here, but food runs the gamut, weighing in at all sizes, shapes, and prices. I've heard that the spice saffron, which is really the carefully harvested inside bits of the crocus flower, is one of the most expensive materials by weight on Earth! And at the other end of the spectrum, there's good old fashioned potatoes and rice. Now I'm hungry, so here's a list of my current faves in no particular order: blueberries, capers, pancakes with chocolate chips and banana chunks, escarole, thick-cut bacon, yellowtail scallion maki, cashew butter, watermelon, hot dogs with all the fixin's, aspara-gus, fresh mozzarella, and french fries.

269. Playing an Instrument

One of life's great joys as far as I'm concerned is playing an instrument, no matter whether you're bound for Carnegie Hall or everyone leaves the room when you start in. You need the instrument itself, but after that you don't need much, just time and patience. I had a friend in college who worked out a schedule where she could play the huge organ in the chapel, and let me tell you that was pretty amazing to go and listen to the sound filling that huge space.

270. Hobbies

Your hobby can be an everyday thing or a once a year indulgence, you can spend pennies or tens of thousands. Collecting things, gardening, biking, reading science fiction, whatever it is, hobbies enhance your life.

271 Meet the Grandparents

One of my son's favorite shows on the PBS Kids channel is called Jakers! *The Adventures of Piggly Winks*, in which a lovable Irish grandfather in the form of a pig recounts his shenanigans as a young farm boy in Ireland. The show always concludes with a segment called "Meet the Grandparents," which finds real children interviewing their grandparents about what the grandparents' childhood was like, and sharing something they can do together. Invariably the grandparents start by saying something like, "When I was a kid, we didn't have television or video games, we had to make up our own fun." And then they show the kids how to make little stilts out of tuna fish cans, or to fashion a doll out of a corn husk (who the heck has corn husks lying around anymore?). But the kids are genuinely enthralled, excited to be spending time with their grandparents and really into the simplest toys.

It's a good lesson to remember: that the imagination can be inspired by limitation. When you grow up in the land before Gameboys, or can't afford one now, you can make the darnedest things into fun that lasts all afternoon. Or even all summer long.

272 Soup

One of my favorite games as a child was called "soup." It was best played after a summer rainstorm, and involved dragging the heavy plastic paint bucket that caught water coming from the gutter over to a rotting tree stump by the driveway. I would then spend hours adding "ingredients" to my soup, and stirring them together with a long stick. The "chicken" was wet bits of wood from the stump, the herbs were grass and leaves, there were some rocks for potatoes, and anything else that caught my fancy. It sounds odd to me now, but it was loads of fun, lemme tell ya.

273–276 Travel

There are so many ways to travel that there's really no excuse for not enjoying it, whatever your means.

273. Armchair Tourist

If you're really broke, you may have to settle for kicking back with a glass of merlot and planning a fantasy vacation to France, complete with library picture books, a few movie rentals (*Amélie, Weekend, The City of Lost Children*), and some homemade crepes.

274. Budget Travel

Or you can travel on a shoestring using the Internet and guidebooks to find hostels, camping, housing exchanges, cheap eats, and the like.

275. Living Abroad

If it fits your lifestyle, why not chuck it all and sublet your apartment or rent out your house, put your stuff in storage, and take off for a while? There are all sorts of ways to do it, from working as a nanny, to couch surfing your way through Europe, to spending the inheritance from your grandma by moving to the old country to the town she was born in (assuming it's not the next town over from yours in the old country of Wisconsin).

276. World-Class Touring

We were just in Sag Harbor, New York, which I'd never been to and found that it more than lives up to its reputation. While we were there, we saw maybe the most incredible yacht I've ever seen, called *Bad Girl*. Chatting with one of the workers on board, we learned that it could be chartered to sail wherever your fancy took you for a mere $250,000 per week. Now that's traveling in style.

277 The Splurge

I don't care what your financial situation is, sometimes you just have to splurge. You set the timetable, but I think if you splurge once a week, the sheen starts to wear off and it doesn't feel special any more. So I'd describe three rules of splurging as:

1. Wait long enough before doing it to really savor it.
2. Surprise yourself with something a bit out of the ordinary.
3. Spend your dough on an item or experience that will have a special place in your memory forever.

278 Trade-off

"Give me the luxuries of life and I will willingly do without the necessities."
— Frank Lloyd Wright

279–283 Luxury

I never believed there could really be that much of a difference between standard and luxury goods until my husband introduced me to high-end shopping (I use the term *shopping* loosely—it's really more like looking and longing). In my opinion, you'd do well to get luxury versions of these things at least once in your life.

279. Leather Shoes

Italian, handcrafted, with good soles. And if you take them to the repair shop every six months, you can probably pass them on to your kid.

280. Handbag

I don't go for the ostentatious logo on the outside (though more power to you if you can pull it off), but have you seen the craftsmanship of these things? The stitching, the lining, the inner pockets? Whew.

281. Winter Coat

You need it, you wear it every day for three months while you walk through slush in the dark, so why not make it special?

282. A Suit and Tie

I have three words for you: tailoring, tailoring, tailoring.

283. Perfume or Cologne

This one's a no-brainer if you divide the cost by how often you wear it and how much pleasure it brings on a daily basis.

284 What to Do with the Overflow

What a wonderful feeling when your cup runneth over. For whatever reason, the bounty is beyond your expectation. You've got a ton of leftovers from Thanksgiving dinner, your cousin is cleaning out her closet that's full of designer clothes, or you got an unexpected year-end bonus at work. My first impulse is to save some for a rainy day, which is all to the good, but not at the expense of using it well or passing some on:

285 Use it Up

What's the point in hoarding (especially where left-overs are concerned)? Throw a big party to share your excess, and bask in glory of it all.

286 Give it Away

If it makes you feel good to have a little extra, imagine those feelings radiating out into the world when you pass it on.

287–290 Permission Granted

I don't know if it's my Midwestern roots (or ruts, as we like to say), but I sometimes catch myself needing a note from home to really enjoy things. Maybe I feel I don't deserve it, or I'm always thinking about what I should be doing instead, but I think it's time to write a permission slip for a lot of things.

287. To Take a Vacation

My dad grew up on a dairy farm, and never took a vacation in his entire childhood. If they went away, who would feed and milk the cows? So, in turn, we never took family vacations when I was a kid, and I still feel a little guilty going off for "no reason." Nobody's milked a cow in my family for twenty-five years; wouldn't you say it's time to let it go?

288. To Have Fun

You're allowed to have fun even when you've got a huge to-do list. Heck, you might even think of a few ways to have fun while you work.

289. To Accept Gifts

My husband is flat out the most generous person I know. And not only that, he doesn't expect anything in return. For many of us this is hard to grasp—that someone could offer every gift they give without a single string attached.

290. To Enjoy What You've Got

No matter what you don't have, or what you think you need, never forget what you've already got and what a source of joy it can be to reinvest yourself in discovering and enjoying what you already have. What are you going to give yourself permission to do? Notice happiness?

291 Comparisons

I've heard people say that you should never compare yourself or your situation to anyone else's. And I do believe that it doesn't do any good to harshly judge your own feelings by comparing your happiness or pain to someone else's. But sometimes it helps to listen to other people's stories to put your feelings in a broader perspective, and to remember that you're not alone, even in your most lonely, desolate moods.

292 Efforts and Results

Sometimes you give it your all and still come up short. Sometimes a well-placed single burst of energy pays huge dividends.

293 The More I Write, the Less I Know

There's a saturation point in all things, when you've put in as much works as it takes to get a thing done, solve a problem, or to make a new discovery, and the last piece of the puzzle is sitting back and letting it happen.

294 Out with the Old

Stuff, stuff, too much stuff! Double stuff may look great on an Oreo, but not so much in your closet. Remember how grand it feels to have spent the day (or in my case I think it'll take a week) clearing out your space? I can work, think, and even sleep better when

I've weeded through, put away, and carted off the excess junk in my life. And you can increase the joy by making money from a garage sale, or by donating a lot of cool useful stuff to people who need it.

eight

Goals and Greatness: Follow
Your Calling (and I Don't Mean How
Many Rollover Minutes You Get)

If you want to live a
happy life, tie it to a goal,
not to people or things.

Albert Einstein

As we struggle through another tough day at work, we may fantasize about how happy we'd be sitting on a beach with a cool drink for the rest of our lives, away from all our responsibilities and family pressures. But deep down we know that the beach would get pretty boring after a week or so, and that we'd miss our familiar loony bin soon enough. I choose to think that Einstein is not talking about short-term goals—filing your taxes on time, getting a raise, winning a race. We sometimes work toward achievements like that with a single-minded mentality: "As soon as I get that raise, I'll be happy." And then each time the desired goal is met, our initial elation is soon replaced by the same nagging feeling of incompleteness; happiness is a carrot dangled just outside of our reach.

The only way to grab that carrot is to live a life that you feel is meaningful and to enjoy the work you choose to do. I'm not promising a life without struggle, but when you have a sense of your own calling you have the means to overcome obstacles and work through menial tasks with a sense of purpose. You may even find the obstacles themselves, and your reaction to them, are another source of satisfaction in your life. Even better, your calling will naturally incorporate the people and things that are most important to you, so you can move beyond linking your sense of well-being to how happy your mother or your spouse is. There's an infinite source of gratification right in front of your face; you just have to reach out and grab it.

295 Ambition Versus Passion

Ambition is the desire to be successful. Passion is intense interest or enthusiasm. My ambition can take me far—it can motivate me to make it to the top. But the end result may feel pretty empty when I get there, because the goal was seeing myself as a success, and once I've done that, what's left? Passion, on the other hand, is ready to explore infinite possibilities. It may or may not lead me to someone else's definition of success, but following my passion elicits a sense of fulfillment that can never dull.

296 The Happy Mechanic

My husband's grandfather tells this story of his early working life. He had trained to be an engineer, and spent long days at the drafting table literally trying not to fall asleep as he worked. He had a talent for engineering, and it paid well. It had a steady track for advancement, and by all accounts was interesting work, so why couldn't he stay awake? Well, part of the problem was that he'd started working in the evenings in a machine shop, and he loved it. For him, nothing could compare to working for hours and hours hunched over an engine. He didn't think it was right to trade life as a respected engineer for an insecure, low-paid, blue-collar job as a mechanic, but that's just what he did. After that he woke up energized every morning, itching to go to work. Soon he had his own forklift business, which grew faster than he could have hoped for, and he built and drove European midget racecars on the side, winning again and again. And to think, the happy mechanic might have been a miserable engineer his whole life.

297 Respect

At one time I worked for one of the most successful men I've ever met. He is a lawyer, author, and crusader for any number of causes. Some of the other people in his firm had the bad habit of "looking through" the support staff—the assistants, mailroom workers, and cleaning crew. My boss was always very attentive to everyone, made a point of introducing himself to new workers, remembered names, and had an easy grace interacting with everyone. It may have been because he grew up poor and had worked his way to the top, but I think it was something deeper. He respected that each person contributes his or her part to the whole. He knew that no one would get anywhere without the synergy of everyone doing their bit with a sense of purpose.

298 A Sense of Purpose

You may think that some work is beneath you, or that people are demeaned by having certain jobs, like scrubbing toilets, fixing cars, or farm work. I'm by no means advocating squalid conditions or workplace injustice, but it's a fact that there are two ways to look at work: people who clean up in schools, for example, may feel demoralized or bitter about doing repetitious work that does not challenge or excite them. But others have found a sense of purpose in what they do. They may feel that they contribute to an essential part of young people's growth by providing a clean and safe environment for learning. The people who embrace this second view will interact with students and teachers in a meaningful way, and will have a greater overall sense of their own worth.

299 Your Own Standard of Success

It can be tough in today's world to have an alternative standard of success. The media bombards us with images of people whom we're told have made it to the top. Our families have their own ideas of what we should do—like when your mother thinks you should be a surgeon. It takes some courage, but defining and pursuing your own standard of success is worth it. Then no matter what your situation looks like to other people, you'll know that you're on the path to the life you've always dreamed about.

300 A Plan for Success

"To achieve great things, two things are needed; a plan, and not quite enough time."

— Leonard Bernstein

301–306 The Ingredients

There's no set recipe for success, but these ingredients certainly can't hurt.

301. Perseverance

Keep at it! There's no better way to succeed, and no other way to know whether you can accomplish what you think you can.

302. Innovation

Redefine the landscape of your field. It can come to you in a moment, but is often the result of a lot of preparation—a miraculous new approach to an old problem.

303. Caring for Others

In simple, everyday ways and in dramatic, save-the-world ways like developing a new vaccine. If helping people is your focus, you can't go wrong.

304. Tackling Challenges

Biting off a little bit more than you think you can chew and pushing through problems as they come.

305. Resilience

Your response to challenges, and never letting difficulty dull your happiness.

306. Faith

Knowing in your heart of hearts that this is *right*.

307 All Used Up

"I want to be thoroughly used up when I die, for the harder I work, the more I live. I rejoice in life for its own sake. Life is no 'brief candle' to me. It is a sort of splendid torch which I have got hold of for the moment, and I want to make it burn as brightly as possible before handing it on to future generations."

— George Bernard Shaw

308 Inspiration

It comes to you in a dream, or from a thoughtful conversation, or just from opening up your eyes and seeing something for the first time. How sweet it is, that spark of imagination!

309 Mind Over Matter

"Most folks are about as happy as they make up their minds to be."

— Abraham Lincoln

310 Happy at Work

What a gift it is to be challenged at work, to be able to take ownership of our projects, and to be inspired and pushed by those around us.

311 Tough Customers

Some people at work are difficult—customers, bosses, employees. Don't let it drain your energy. Figure out the minimum contact you can have, make it as pleasant as possible, and move on. Don't let anybody sap your energy.

312 Easy

The happiest people I know face challenges willingly, with a strength and energy I admire, and they end up growing in their careers and as human beings as a result. Others rarely push themselves, doing variations on the same simple tasks over and over to make themselves feel good and look smart. Seems to me the short-term comfort of easy success isn't worth the price of long-term stagnation.

313 The Complicated Monster Under the Bed

I had a friend who started going to therapy with a host of what she thought were intricate, deep-seated problems. The therapist was able to quickly find the root of the problem, and the simplicity of the solution stunned my friend. The solution wouldn't be easy to implement, but the problem itself was not a big scary monster under the bed. Sometimes we want to keep our problems complicated because we're invested in an image of ourselves in constant struggle with an unbeatable obstacle. Or we're more terrified of the solution because it probably requires change on our part, so we convince ourselves it's too complex to solve. Happiness might be closer than you think—try asking for help from someone whose opinion you respect, and really listen to what they say. They might see the bigger picture more clearly, and help you on your way to solving your problem.

314 The Finish Line

What feels sweeter than setting the course, gathering your gear, starting your race, climbing those hills, and finally, finally making it to the finish line? Maybe the only thing sweeter is gearing up for your next course.

315 Chosen

You often hear amazing, satisfied, courageous people say, "I had no idea I would be doing what I'm doing today. My life chose me."

316 Step Aside, Left Brain

How can your life choose you? People may think it's luck or happenstance when opportunities knock on their door (or knock them down flat). But I believe that to make choices that will effect your life for the better, you must relinquish control. You must find a frame of mind from which you can make real choices, and that requires that you be in the moment, ready to evaluate the facts of your life honestly. One problem that many of us overachievers face is our ability to plan and organize *ad nauseum.* We're relying too heavily on our left brain, which makes lists and generates orderly outcomes. Sometimes we have to put a muzzle on our efficient left brain and let loose the messy trouble-maker, the right brain. Put on some music, make a drawing of your problem without using any words, or try a solution you think might be out of your reach. The right brain takes creative leaps of imagination, sees the bigger picture, and is the compass that can help you choose your life.

317 The Paradox of Control and Choice

When you're all about control, the only choices you can make are choices that will help you maintain your sense of control. You are a slave to your own need to predict the future. The only way to make real, unfettered choices is to relinquish the need to know every possible outcome of the choices you make.

Put it this way. You're ready to find your calling, something that's fulfilling now and grows into something just as fulfilling later. Your conscious mind could never predict what that calling is and what your future life will look like. It cannot map out every step that will get you there. If you tried, your map would by a series of to-do's, and no matter how much imagination you put into them, there would always be something missing. So ease up on the control pedal, and feel the exhilaration of the unknown.

318 Structured Freedom

When I was a kid, I went to an alternative elementary school where there were no classrooms, and from the age of seven, kids set their own schedule and completed tasks on their own. There was a huge play structure that everyone wanted to be on, and the only rules for being there were that you had to have something to read and you had to be quiet. Let me tell you, reading was pretty popular. The whole thing might have looked like anarchy to a traditionalist, but the kids, teachers, and parents all saw the value of a little structured freedom.

319 Obstacles

"Man needs difficulties; they are necessary for health."
— Carl Gustav Jung

320 Little Rewards

When you have a long and difficult task, reward your-self at every step. Not with a shopping spree or a new car, but with an apple, or a walk, or a piece of dark chocolate.

321 Lifelong Learning

What a wonderful luxury to have the time to read and write as a daily practice. How cool is it that we can go back to school, or just take a class, any time we want?

322 Good News

My father used to tell the story of hearing me returning home from kindergarten one day. He could hear me coming from out in the yard, and I was screaming my head off. Thinking something was wrong, he rushed outside to find me as I yelled, "Daddy! Daddy! I can read, I can read!!!"

323 Accomplishments

I don't remember how tough it was to learn to read, or talk, or to button buttons, and I just have a dim sense of struggling to learn to tie my shoes. But I know that big accomplishments start small, and that's pretty cool.

324 Ownership

"The best years of your life are the ones in which you decide your problems are your own. You do not blame them on your mother, the ecology, or the president. You realize that you control your own destiny."

— Albert Ellis

325 What to Tackle

We've all got a list of problems a mile long, and the solutions range from making a quick phone call to sticking with a diet and exercise plan from here on out. But what about the things that don't have solutions? Or that you can't solve in the present moment, for whatever reason? Why are they still eating up space on your list? Whether it's on paper or in your head, sort your list to rid it of the things you can't change. Or rephrase your problems into ones that you can actually make a stab at. You'll feel physically lighter and renewed to tackle the rest of your list.

326 Delicate Balance

I find it hard sometimes to find the balance between maintaining my convictions and staying open to new things. I imagine I'm on a seesaw by myself, standing right in the middle. Lean too far one way, and I'm immersed in my own rigidity, and nothing can change my mind. Stumble back the other way, and I'm in a free fall, with so many ideas and thoughts coming at me I can't keep my foothold. Balancing right in the center takes a lot of strength and a little bit of fancy footwork. By constantly shifting my weight a little this way and a little that, I'll stay on my feet for sure.

327–329 The Gift of Failure

327. "Learn from the mistakes of others. You can't live
live long enough to make them all yourself."

— Eleanor Roosevelt

328. "Failures are finger posts on the road to achievement."

— C. S. Lewis

329. "I didn't fail the test, I just found 100 ways to do
it wrong."

— Benjamin Franklin

330 Commitment

It's always inspiring to me to see someone give their
all. A professional athlete in mid-air, a chef hovering
over a perfect pastry with intense concentration. Or
even nonhuman effort—a racehorse, or a search-and-
rescue dog. Commitment is exciting.

331 Bravery

What if I told you it's better to face the worst than to protect yourself from the sort-of bad? I know, you don't believe me. Neither do I, a lot of the time. But it's still true.

332 Magic

"Whatever you do, or dream you can, begin it. Boldness has genius and power and magic in it."
— Johann Wolfgang von Goethe

333 Out on a Limb

Here's to all the people in the world whose passion and persistence takes them to the edge of something new. And here's to finding the courage to jump. And here's to flying for the first time.

the end

Plain as the Nose
on Your Face

We choose our joys
and sorrows long before
we experience them.

Kahlil Gibran

Happiness as By-product

A strange thing happened as I wrote this book. I've been particularly moody, alternating between crabby and elated, and it took me a while to figure out why. I was trying too hard!

The harder you try to make yourself happy, or the more you focus on "being happy" for its own sake, without connecting it to actions in your life, the more it eludes you. It's like trying to win a game of tennis by clutching your racket and thinking only about winning. You're surely going to flub some shots, and miss some opportunities, because you're in the state of mind to *win win win* the game, when you'd fare much better in a *play play play* mindset. Focus on winning takes you away from the relaxed, energetic state you need to be in to complete the actions necessary to win: serving well, hitting volleys, coming to the net.

How's this for the name of a scientific study? "The Pursuit and Assessment of Happiness Can Be Self-Defeating."* In this study volunteers were asked

* J. W. Schooler, D. Ariely, and G. F. Lowenstein, in *The Psychology of Economic Decisions: Rationality and Well-Being.* Oxford University Press.

to listen to Stravinsky's *Rite of Spring*. Some were asked to just listen, while others were asked to focus on consciously trying to be happy. As it turns out, the ones who were trying to be happy ended up feeling worse than the ones who just listened. Does this spell the end for happiness mongers like myself? Well, no. All it means is that we have to chill out and stop trying so hard. It means we just have to listen to the music without expectation and without planning our responses. Yet there I was, pursuing and assessing, pursuing and assessing, pursuing and assessing and . . . self-defeating, more often than not.

Happiness is all around us. We can't create it and we can't micromanage it. You can't force yourself to be happier. You can only discover it. The best way I know to do that is to put yourself in the path of happy accidents by doing what you love with purpose and staying open and aware to the possibility of happiness beyond your wildest dreams.

I was on a walk the other day and encountered a huge rose bush covered in clusters of pink blossoms just behind a fence. Without thinking about it, I went up and got closer, but I couldn't smell much. Darn these roses, I thought, darn my nose. But now I was determined. I smashed my face up against the fence and stuck my nose right in the middle of a flower and was rewarded with the lightest, cleanest scent you can imagine. The absorbing sounds and smells of the city outside fell away for a moment, and my whole world was rose, rose, rose. I walked away with a fence-shaped impression on my face and the lingering happiness of losing myself in the moment.

Pass It On

"Thousands of candles can be lit from a single candle, and the life of the candle will not be shortened. Happiness never decreases by being shared."

— Buddha

The single most important action you can take when it comes to happiness is spreading it around. Happiness never decreases by being shared; in fact it often increases exponentially as it travels from one person to another. If you can light up the lives of everyone you meet, think of how many thousands of candles that will be. Think of how much lighter the world will be.

Down to the Seeds

My father used to eat an apple all the way down to the seeds and the stem. He would finish off every edible piece, even the core. That's the way to live, it seems to me.

about the author

Addie Johnson, who grew up in Minnesota and San Francisco, went east to Vassar College and stayed put in New York. She's an actor and helps run Rising Phoenix Rep, a small developmental theatre company. She's also an editor and writer, and the author of *The Little Book of Big Excuses*, Conari, 2007. She lives in Brooklyn with her family who help her remember every day that life is sweet.

to our readers

Conari Press, an imprint of Red Wheel/Weiser, publishes books on topics ranging from spirituality, personal growth, and relationships to women's issues, parenting, and social issues. Our mission is to publish quality books that will make a difference in people's lives—how we feel about ourselves and how we relate to one another. We value integrity, compassion, and receptivity, both in the books we publish and in the way we do business.

Our readers are our most important resource, and we value your input, suggestions, and ideas about what you would like to see published. Please feel free to contact us, to request our latest book catalog, or to be added to our mailing list.

Conari Press

An imprint of Red Wheel/Weiser, LLC

500 Third Street, Suite 230

San Francisco, CA 94107

www.redwheelweiser.com